Hertford Within Living Memory

Compiled by the Hertfordshire
Federation of Women's Institutes from notes
sent by Institutes in the County

Published jointly by
Countryside Books, Newbury
and the HFWI, St Albans

COUNTRYSIDE BOOKS
3, Catherine Road,
Newbury, Berkshire

ISBN 1 85306 201 4

Designed by Mon Mohan
Produced through MRM Associates Ltd, Reading
Printed in England by J.W. Arrowsmith Ltd, Bristol

Contents

Acknowledgements

Hertfordshire Federation of Women's Institutes would like to thank all W.I. members ('Hertfordshire Hedgehogs') who supplied material for this project through their local Institutes.

Unfortunately we were not able to include extracts from every submission; to do so would have meant some duplication of content, and of course we had to take into account the total amount of space available in the book.

But all the contributions, without exception, were of value in deciding the shape and content of the book. We are grateful for them all.

Finally, our thanks are due to Mrs P Challenger for the delightful sketches and to the Hitchin Museum for their help with the photographs, and for supplying the cover picture.

Eve Davis
Co-ordinator

List of Contributing WIs

ABBOTS LANGLEY
ALDBURY
ARDELEY
ASHWELL
BALDOCK & CLOTHALL
BAYFORD
BEDMOND
BERKHAMSTED
BERKHAMSTED CASTLE
BOREHAMWOOD
BOVINGDON
BOXMOOR
BRAUGHING
BRICKET WOOD
BROOKMANS PARK
BUNTINGFORD
CHILDWICK GREEN
CHORLEYWOOD
CODICOTE
DIGSWELL
ESSENDON
FELDEN
FLAMSTEAD END
FLAUNDEN
GREAT AMWELL
HARPENDEN VILLAGE
HERTINGFORDBURY
HIGH CROSS & THUNDRIDGE
HINXWORTH & EDWORTH
HUNSDON
HUNTON BRIDGE
ICKLEFORD
KIMPTON
KINGSBURY
KNEBWORTH Evening
LETCHWORTH

LEVERSTOCK GREEN
LITTLE GADDESDEN
LITTLE MUNDEN
MARDLEY HEATH
MUCH HADHAM
NASH MILLS
NEW MILL
NORTHAW
OFFLEY
OLD STEVENAGE
PANSHANGER
REDBOURN
ROE GREEN
ST ALBANS CITY
ST MARGARETS Evening
SANDRIDGE
SARRATT
SHENLEY
SOUTH HARPENDEN
SOUTH MIMMS
THE AYOTS
THE CAUSEWAY
WALKERN
WATERFORD
WATTON-AT-STONE
WELHAM GREEN
WELWYN
WESTMILL
WESTWICK
WHEATHAMPSTEAD
WIGGINTON
WILDHILL
WOODHALL
WOOLMER GREEN
WORMLEY
WYMONDLEY

The County of
Hertfordshire

St. Albans Abbey

LETCH

HITCHIN

HARPENDEN

M.1.

HEMEL
HEMPSTEAD

ST. ALBANS

M.10

M.25

WATFORD

RICKMANSWORTH

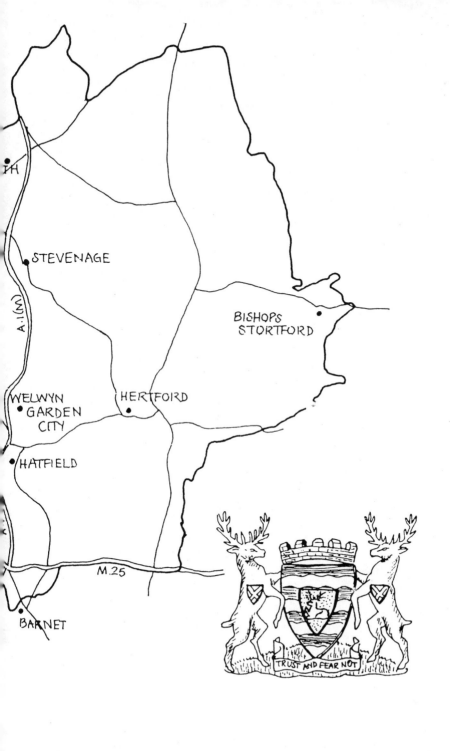

Foreword

We are frequently told that we should not live in the past! Maybe so – but equally we must not lose sight of the past as so much of what we are, what we do and what we see about us have their origins in the past.

The human memory is not always the most reliable of filing systems – with the passing of each successive generation recollections can become highly coloured, blurred or may fade out of sight altogether.

This book, a compilation of reminiscences, written by members of the Hertfordshire Federation of Women's Institutes, endeavours to halt this deterioration by setting out in print those innumerable interesting facts, stories and snippets from our past which otherwise could be all too easily lost forever. Not only that – it is very likely that as you turn the pages and read the contributors' memories it will stir your own and you too may say 'Do you know, I well remember . . .'

Jean Curl
County Chairman

TOWN & COUNTRY LIFE

TOWNS OLD AND NEW

Hertfordshire has examples of both old and new – towns that have grown through the centuries and towns that represent the thinking behind the 'Garden City' concept that first blossomed at the end of the 19th century. These memories are just a flavour of life in our towns in the past decades.

WATFORD AND RICKMANSWORTH REMEMBERED

'My first encounter with Hertfordshire was in 1927 in Watford, just prior to my tenth birthday. Watford in the 1920s was a thriving market town, reputed to be the richest in the county. Clarendon Road was known as Millionaires Row. The pond on the Parade was a place where horses used to go to drink. Watford market was held each side of Market Street in the High Street, the stalls being lit by naphtha lamps. Fishers the butcher's sold meat off cheap on a Saturday evening, a joint of lamb costing one shilling and sixpence, enough for Sunday lunch, Sunday supper and cold for Monday with bubble and squeak.

Our first home was a room in Longspring, our final house in Gammons Lane. Gas lamps the lighting, candles to bed and a kitchen range for warming the living room. The latter had to be blackleaded once a week and the flues swept out.

Dad worked as a lorry driver for Tom Simmons whose office was in Market Street; it was a haulier's business. Mother had a job in Delectaland, a chocolate and biscuit firm in Sandown Road. The best part of her work was when she used to bring home damaged chocolates.

Schooling was at Callowland Girls School. On Tuesday and Friday we attended Alexandra School to learn how to be cooks and housewives. In the laundry room the flat irons were heated on a large black stove with ridges on it to lodge the irons on. Damask tablecloths had to be pressed until they were polished.

Sunday school days were at the Salvation Army, and outings meant trips to Bricket Wood and Chipperfield, with games and races in a field. Tea was buns and lemonade, and we all returned tired but happy.'

'I was born in Rickmansworth, a town served by both canal and railways. We lived very near the Batchworth Locks and setting out for the town always took us over the bridge. As a child of the 1940s the canals at that time were still very busy. Rickmansworth was a good stop for the canal folk. The women shopped at the Canal Stores run by a Mrs King. It was our local "little" shop and the first shop I was allowed to go to on my own. There always seemed to be canal women in long dresses in the shop who looked far too large to fit into the narrow boats they lived on, together with numerous children. The shop always had crusty new bread on sale and during the pickling season I was sent with a bottle to buy the vinegar which came from a big barrel with a tap. Milk churns were also kept there for people to collect their milk. However, we had ours delivered by horse and cart driven by a lady whose shape looked very much like a very tall milk churn with a chopped off haircut.

Another attraction on the canal were the stables. By the locks and bridge were big stables for the horses. All the barges were pulled by horses and it was fun to peep inside to see all the goings on with these huge animals. One night in the late 1940s there was a terrible fire which burnt out the biggest building and some horses lost their

Horse drawn barges were to be seen on Hertfordshire's canals, such as this one on the canal at Boxmoor.

lives. As a small child it left me with a few sleepless nights and a smell in my mind that has never left me.

A short walk along the towpath brought one opposite Walkers Yard where among other things they manufactured motor narrowboats. Always busy and plenty to watch from across the canal during the school holidays.

Rickmansworth's claim to fame railwaywise was the fact that on the Metropolitan line, the engine was changed from an electric one out of London to a steam engine to continue the journey towards Chorleywood and beyond. My future husband lived in Chorleywood and our good-night kisses on the doorstep were ruled by this changeover. Warning came from the electric engine from London with a whistle as it approached Ricky station. A quick final kiss and a four minute dash to the station, the time it took for the engine changeover.

My brother's schooldays were ruled by Ricky's other railway line. The little station, as it was known locally, was the terminus for a branch that ran to Watford Junction until the early 1950s. It was not unknown for the driver to hang on for him to do his one minute dash from the house if he was late in the morning. On occasion Mum took my sister and me to Watford on this line for special shopping trips.

During my school holidays, I worked at a grocer's (pre-supermarket days), a well respected "High Class Family Grocer". An establishment my mother approved of because the customers were the gentry of the district so I would not become corrupted! A far cry from the Canal Stores and its vinegar from the barrel – here it was sold in bottles! Here were fine wines, cheeses other than cheddar, a range of coffee beans (I used to love using the grinder) and a newcomer to coffee for the masses, Nescafe Instant at three shillings and sixpence for a small tin. Biscuits except for very fancy boxes were sold loose, as was all the dried fruit, great sticky cases of glace cherries, candied peel, sultanas and raisins. It was the only Christmas Day I couldn't bear the sight of pudding, cake and mince pies. Most of the business was done by delivery van. Customers either phoned or ordered at the counter and the goods were delivered later.'

THE GARDEN CITIES

'The first Garden City, Letchworth, gets its name from a small old village. As it was developed houses were rented before the roads were surfaced. People came from afar to start a new life here. The factories were built to one side of town, this was planned to allow everyone to be in a garden environment.

The factories themselves had gardens and were maintained by true gardeners. Workers cycled from villages all

13

round, quite a sight first thing in the morning to see them arrive from all directions. Later buses arrived.

There was a small library but sadly a lot of the original buildings have gone, the first picture house, swimming pool and several social halls, where concerts were performed by local musicians etc. Most things were sold at your door, horse-drawn carts brought paraffin, candles, gas mantles, soda, all things considered necessary for cleaning, bread, milk and greengrocery. Old ladies came with baskets selling lace and pegs, etc. There was every denomination of religion represented, Quakers being one of the first. St Paul's was built in stages when funds allowed.

Life was very hard for some people, including my father invalided from the First World War, and families were large. Shops were interesting, mostly run by elderly "ladies". We had Maypole, where we bought butter cut from a large square and patted into one pound shapes with butter pats kept in water, quite fascinating. There was a secondhand furniture store which was allowed to display all sorts of knick-knacks on the pavement. The Wynd housed a real old fashioned book shop owned by a real old gentleman. The two Miss Welches had a lovely little haberdashery shop. We had dress shops where you could walk around and your money was put in a container fixed to wires, a handle was pulled and off it whizzed to a secret destination and returned with your change.

In the 1920s the local wheelwright walked round the village with his ladder lighting the street lamps. The local sweet shop sold toffee on a tray broken with a hammer and oh, those large slabs of Cadbury's chocolate on the very top shelf, which I promised myself when I was rich.'

'My first memories of Hertfordshire are when my parents moved from Essex to Welwyn Garden City in 1928 when I was twelve years old. The town was then in the first stages of development and we were surrounded by green fields and country lanes. To me this was idyllic, as I had been brought up in a London suburb and was not allowed to play in the street. I soon made friends at school and can recall playing in the fields and gathering wild flowers and going for long country walks.

Welwyn Stores was the only shop as everything belonged to Welwyn Garden City Ltd, including the bakery, laundry, builders etc, so with no competition it was an expensive place in which to live.'

'My parents went to live in Welwyn Garden City in 1920 when there were some 50 people there. I was born in 1922 in a London nursing home, there being no such facilities in Welwyn Garden City. My mother brought me home by train when I was two weeks old. She was concerned for my health in the seven smoky tunnels, but I survived and have loved trains ever since, especially steam ones.

Childhood was happy – we had no car or wireless and anywhere we went had to be on foot, by bike or possibly train or bus. We made our own entertainment and thought life was full.

Swimming at Stanborough pool was a cold ordeal – the pool was just a portion of the river then, and one was inclined to swallow a fish or tadpole at times. Father wore a one-piece bathing costume – navy blue, buttoned on the shoulders and as he emerged from the pool the costume grew longer and longer until it reached his ankles.

In those days before there was much development in the Garden City, the commuters went to the station in wellingtons, as there was one muddy field to cross. On reaching the station, wellington boots were thrown in a heap and respectable shoes donned, the process being reversed in the evening.'

'My memories of Hemel Hempstead begin in 1952 when we migrated to Hemel Hempstead New Town to live in a new house and give our three daughters a cleaner and healthier environment than London.

Crossing where the now famous Magic Roundabout is situated, had sometimes to be achieved only on the bus as the Gade often flooded the area. I remember sheltering under the trees in Gadebridge Park during a slight shower and seeing the children's delight at the seemingly masses of frogs leaping about from the watercress beds. We delighted in walking through the country lanes on a warm Sunday evening to sit in the garden of an old public house to have crisps and ginger beer before returning home. There was a street party to celebrate the Queen's Coronation in 1953. The Queen later visited the New Town, hence the square in Adeyfield was renamed the Queen's Square.

In those early days you could see the men running down the road, sometimes with their ties in their hands, to catch the firm's coach to London at 6am as the factories had not all moved out here.

COUNTRY VILLAGES AND NEW ESTATES

Fetching water from the well or milk from the farm, travelling by pony and trap, walking down dusty country lanes lined by flower-filled hedgerows – memories which are not so far distant for Hertfordshire's rural villages. Yet at the same time, the county's proximity to London meant that new estates were being built to house the capital's overflow population and newcomers to Hertfordshire were struggling to create communities of their own.

OUR VILLAGE

This description of Bedmond was written in the 1920s. "Bedmond is the name of our little village and we are very proud of it. It is situated on hills and although it is very old fashioned it is very pretty.

In many ways it remains much the same as 50 years ago – the pond then was much larger than it is now and during the summer months people came from miles around to fish in it. In the winter there was skating by lantern light, these lights made of swedes with candles placed in them.

The farmers used to bring their flocks of sheep to be washed there which indeed was a very pretty sight. Porridge Pot Hill is another noted place, for there the old witches lived in a little wooden hut. The hut I saw but not the witches.

When St Albans Abbey was being restored, gravel was got from a field nearby, which is now called Church Hill, since a church has been built on it.

In those days people were very industrious, nearly everyone used to bake their own bread, but now the bakehouses have been turned into washhouses. Making hats and straw plaiting was another industry which nearly every woman did in those days and in the evening when the menfolk came home they helped too; when a dozen hats had been made the enormous sum of tenpence or a shilling was given in return.

After the infants school was built a night school for men was started, but now they have a reading room and we women have something too and that is an institute. We make all sorts of things with raffia which is a very interesting pastime. We are trying very hard to get a village hall of our own, where we can hold our meetings. When we have got that we shall think we have done something worth doing for our little village of Bedmond.

Bedmond has something to be proud of as it is mentioned in history as the home of Nicholas Breakspear, the only Englishman to become a Pope. Just behind the Breakspear Farm is a little Holy Well and many barrels of water have been taken from it and sent to London hospitals as it is supposed to possess wonderful healing properties.

On 13th June 1925 a pageant in memory of Breakspear was held in the grounds of Breakspear Farm and to many of us it was a day never to be forgotten. We don't have to walk the miles we used to as now we have buses in our little village of Bedmond."

Today Wigginton, high on the Chilterns, is a commuter village but in my childhood days the majority of the menfolk worked locally on the farms, large estates and local brickworks. For what reason I do not know, but most of them seemed to have a nickname. There was Ookey, Washer, Cogger, Pussey, Tiggly, Flukey, Cheddar and Chicken, Flashman, Shadey, Dyedy and Giggle. In some cases the wives were known by the nickname too, such as Rose Chicken and Lisa Cheddar.'

'We had a blacksmith's shop at Essendon before the war, where they used to make all the shoes for the horses. You could also stand inside by the big fire watching them make the clips and shoe the horses.

You could take your milk can and get it full for only twopence from Mr and Mrs Starkess. There was also a small shed on top of Essendon Hill where the men could go and get their suits made to their liking for a small fee. The man used to sit all day on a stool making these suits.

He could just be seen through a small window. In the village there was a baker's, where you could buy lovely fresh bread and also see it baked. There was also a cobbler who worked from a small shed. There was the old village water pump placed at the entrance of Church Cottages. This pump was very much used. Around 1944 in our village reading room, the village men and women worked on radio parts for Conrad. There was a tin chapel in those days at the top of 6 The Terrace garden.'

'I have childhood memories of going with my mother to the paddling pool in Letchworth. Letchworth – the first Garden City – it must have seemed like heaven to my parents coming from smoky, crowded London after the Great War. It had well planned streets, lined with trees and all the factories were together in one area. It also had a baby clinic – almost unheard of in the 1920s. Then in 1937 we moved to Baldock, a very small market town but on the Great North Road and so very busy.

I remember Simpson's Brewery and standing outside watching the huge dray horse with his cart filled with bags of grain, which were winched up and then disappeared through a door at the top of the building.

We had a farm at the end of our gas-lit lane and every day a herd of cows would be herded along for milking – I remember one day, someone forgot to shut our gate and we had cows in the front garden!'

'When I was a child and living in Aldbury there were five shops, a shoemaker and two laundries. Our water had to be fetched from wells; there was a building in a local garden, one half a wellhouse and the other half a bakehouse. Local men made their living by working on farms, although a few worked in a brick kiln. Just outside the village was a fever hospital, and there was also a small nursing home which was just behind the local shop.'

'I can so well remember the delights of discovering life in a village, when we moved to Hatfield in 1923 when I was twelve years old.

After the noise and bustle of north west London, I felt life was one long holiday, with fields and hedges and trees all round. We lived in Newtown House, a Victorian 16 roomed place, standing in an acre of garden. It is now demolished with other houses, cottages, shops and little alleyways that made up the Newtown part of Hatfield, and is now White Lion Square. Pretty French Horn Lane wound its way down to the old village of Hatfield, with Holier's Dairy on the way, where milk was delivered in horse-drawn floats.

Nearby was where Miss Caeser held her private junior school for the children of the fourth Marquess and Marchioness of Salisbury and the local doctors. Her sister was a portrait painter, they were both very tall, elegant ladies always smiling.

Lower down is old Rectory Drive, where lived several distinguished families; branching off is Cranborne Road which was then a footpath through allotments to the station, known as the garden fields. The sun always seemed to be shining there on masses of flowers and vegetables. The lane went past fields and Glebeland Cottages, which are still there, down to the old gas works, by the railway bridge which carries the main line trains from London to Edinburgh. Under the bridge the lane divided with "Triangle House" in the middle. There lived a well loved Dr Brittain, quite a character in his way. He was renowned for driving an old Morris Cowley car which never seemed to be cleaned, and for many instances of not sending in his bills to patients. His practice even spread to St Albans.

The left fork of the lane was Batterdale with more cottages and the Carmelite convent. I remember when we school children saw our first "wedding" there of a young girl "taking the veil". That building later became a factory!

After more interesting places, was the fire station where Batterdale met the London/Great North Road. The right fork continued down to the main road with more houses and cottages where lived another well known character, Daisy Gray.

Hatfield Park was and still is a lovely place to roam around in. We could walk up to the Home Farm dairy to get cheap skimmed milk, which the children carried home in little oval-lidded cans.

Spring time brought wonderful spreads of daffodils and we were allowed to pick one bunch each. The eagle eye of the lodgekeeper was always on the lookout for any more hidden in prams or under coats.

"Wooding time" was when we were allowed to drag home any fallen logs or branches of trees for our home fires. That was real hard work. I was rather envious of those children who were released from school lessons to help the farmers during the potato digging time – "Spud 'ocking" they called it.'

'In 1925 there were eleven public houses in Leverstock Green and the Red Lion, now a private house, was the biggest. The women of the village did straw-plaiting for the hat industry and someone used to walk to Luton to deliver it. Eventually a post office and shop opened, while the cobbler and the undertaker worked from their homes. The blacksmith attracted junior school children on their way home and they were allowed to stay in the doorway to watch. Milk was delivered by horse and cart and measured into a jug. The village used to have a pond – responsible for at least one death by drowning. Now we have a parade of shops, a village hall and a library but no cobbler, no undertaker, no blacksmith, no village pond and only two public houses.'

'I was born in Digswell in 1923 in a cottage by the bridge which was over the river Mimram. At that time the only water we could use was from the river for washing etc and drinking water was from a spring which was situated on the river edge; we had to go over the bridge, through a gate, down a small path to get our drinking water from the spring. Later on our house was bought by Mr Frank Wells, son of H G Wells the writer. There was not a lot of traffic that went through Digswell at this time, mostly horses and carts. The baker used to come round by horse and cart delivering bread and cakes. The horses used to go to the blacksmith's to be shod, which was just across the road from our house. I spent many hours there watching the blacksmith at work. Our milk came from Tewin Water farm, it was twopence for four pints and we fetched it in a jug. There was a lane which went towards Welwyn Garden City, which at this time was nearly all fields and farms. Further up the road there was a footpath which led to a small place called Blackfan; it only consisted of four houses but my friends used to come there to St John's school every day. Our village school held 100 pupils, they came from Burnham Green, Harmer Green, Digswell and Blackfan. My aunts and uncles attended the school before me as most of my family were born in Hertfordshire.

At Tewin Water House lived Sir Otto Beit, and every year on Boxing Day, they held a meet of the foxhounds, it was lovely to go and see the huntsmen and the hounds. Tewin Water House is now a school for deaf children.'

'Village life in Essendon in the 1940s was simple but good. We loved to visit the blacksmith to help Mr Hewitt with the horses. Then we children would go on to the local farm to help in the cowshed, or potato picking, thistle dodging or even bale carting with the land girls who lodged in the village. The village had four grocer's shops, one butcher's and a post office, two petrol stations, three pubs and one hotel, a working men's club, a tea shop, a cyclists' rest, shoe repairs, a builder's yard and a funeral yard. There were football, cricket and tennis clubs, and darts, skittles and domino tournaments at the local pubs. There was a very good bus service too, the 342 running hourly between New Barnet and Bishops Stortford, and at the bottom of the hill the 341 from Hertford to St Albans.

All the men seemed to have nicknames, Cudgel (my dad), Marrow, Mousy, Weasel, Stouty, Ratty, Duster, Dordy, Shirty, Dingel, Chex, Towny, Bomber, Rushy, Gunner, Hi Hi, Nine O'clock, Ocker, Zooet, Tinger – what a privilege to have known all these characters.'

'As in most villages, pubs abounded at the Ayots for the farmers and estate labourers – not only the Red Lion and The Wagoners – still in existence, but also the Horse and Jockey on the Green, now a private house, and the Brocket Arms in Ayot St Lawrence – now a very fashionable establishment. Older residents still remember Miss Jessie Bott, the very resolute teacher of Ayot St Peter primary school, which finally closed in 1948. There was also a village shop and post office in both Ayots, the one in Ayot Green presided over by Dolly Fever, always dressed in black and a positive tartar for putting the fear of God into all the children. It sold everything from groceries to garden tools and sadly closed down about twelve years ago.

In Ayot St Lawrence most early memories go back to George Bernard Shaw – a domineering influence on the village with the famous visitors he received. But he was also a rather eccentric and crotchety old man – for many years a widower – who rarely participated in village activities. One village function which he did attend produced one of his famous bon mots – when his housekeeper asked him on his return, "Did you enjoy yourself,

Mr Shaw?" he replied, "Of course I did, since there was nothing else to enjoy." However, in a quiet way he did contribute to village life – he donated a beautiful pair of wrought iron gates to the old ruined church and cemetery, which were stolen in 1991. Another excitement, well remembered, was the arrival of King Michael of Roumania, taking up exiled residence in Ayot House during the Second World War. Fancy having a King living in our midst – even an ex one!'

ESTATE VILLAGES

'Mr William Baker MP, wealthy merchant and Alderman of the City of London, and his family were the last owners of Bayford village. The village comprised several large houses, some farms and many small cottages. The Baker family improved the estate and were the chief benefactors to the parish. They built Bayfordbury, a large mansion to the north of the village, surrounding it with an ornamental park. Many trees were planted, huge cedars in front of the house, several woods including a fine collection of rare conifers, and a Pinetum filled with exotic pines. The Baker family replaced the old parish church, provided a school with a bequest from Charlotte Baker and presented the village with a memorial hall in 1913. This provided Bayford with a heritage largely preserved today with the village hall the centre of many local functions.

Nearly all the men and women worked on the estate, either farming, as woodmen, keeping up repairs on the "big house", or repairing the farms and cottages on the estate. Women were able to work at the larger houses, and the village had its own dressmaker too. The milkman delivered daily, the butcher came to us twice a week and the baker three times. These all came by horse-drawn carts, and at lunchtime while the tradesman had a quick lunch, the horse had a nosebag of hay.

We were a close community who helped one another through life and enjoyed the simple pleasures of fairs, fetes and parties. Our landlords were particularly good ones. Mrs Clinton-Baker and her husband were the very last to own the house. She was president of the local WI and travelled round by horse and cart to visit the villagers if they were ill, bringing soup with her.'

'Lady Ela Russell, eldest daughter of the Ninth Duke of Bedford, built and lived at Chorleywood House until she died. The following are a few reminiscences told to me by a resident of Chorleywood whose father worked for her Ladyship in the late 1920s and 1930s.

"At first we lived in the Fishery Cottage on the Chess where my father, who was an under-gardener, looked after the waterwheel which was used to feed Chorleywood House with water and light. He was also one of the woodsmen. The cottage had a fishing room and a boat which he could take out on to the river. Later we moved up to the Lodge. I found Lady Ela very kind to me as a small boy (I was born in 1923), I think because I had auburn hair as she did. When my brother and I were ill she would send us presents. She often asked me to accompany her on walks round the estate and farm and always rewarded me with sixpence at the end.

In those days the estate had quite a large farm with cows, pigs, chickens, a bull and donkeys. The donkeys were used to draw the cart in which she would drive about. They were also used to pull the mowing machine to cut the lawns and sometimes they came to a full stop and refused to go any further. There were many outdoor staff to look after the farm and gardens. The gardens were full of flowers. There were two ponds and avenues of trees, some of which are still there today. At the side of the house is a sunken garden and Lady Ela had a favourite seat where she sat in summer. I used to have to take the post up to the house from the Lodge, going to the back door of course, and touching my cap to the parlour maid. The Duchess of Bedford (the one who was lost in her airplane) sometimes came to visit and she liked me to walk her up the drive to the house and back to her car. I liked her very much and she always rewarded me with a shilling. When Lady Ela died in February 1936 at the age of 81, she lay in state in her bedroom on the first floor guarded by four of her staff until the funeral. Her ashes now lie in the Bedford Chapel at Chenies."'

SOUTHDOWN

'Southdown adjoins Harpenden and was known when I was born in 1912 as the Bowling Alley. At one end is the famous Skew Bridge which was built by local labour drawn from the farms around to take the railway line through on the old Midland Railway line. Farm labourers were paid miserably badly in the 19th century and they were glad to leave the land and earn better money. Next to the bridge was the gas works and showroom. Two cottages stood back just before the Plough and Harrow pub, with a coffee room, a small school and the tin chapel. After that, allotments and pea fields and cornfields stretched all the way to the PAX factory where rubber heels were made with a hole in the middle so that they could be turned round to get the maximum wear out of them! Next to the factory was a storm water pond which also received all the dirty water from the factory and it is still there surrounded by a wall and railings and largely hidden from sight, though all around has changed completely.

There was a hat factory called Fields in Southdown employing over 100 people. There was also a basket factory in Kingcroft Road. The Bates family kept the post

Cravells Road, Harpenden c1915, a quiet road typical of many in the days before the motor car became commonplace.

office for many years with a printing works at the back. There was a shoe shop, haberdasher's, grocery store and butcher's, all locally owned. There were some very poor cottages on the other side of the road by the Skew Bridge.

At the bottom of Cravells Road were just four cottages. Mr Westward the corn merchant had a wooden shed behind there with huge bins filled with maize, wheat, mixed corn and all sorts of feed stuff. He used to weigh it all out into hundredweight sacks on huge scales and we children used to beg him to weigh us. He always said he hadn't the time, but just as we were about to leave, he used to relent and say, "Oh, all right get on the scales and I'll weigh you." He was lovely.

We kept chickens and it was my job to carry home the bags of chicken feed. By the time I got home I was covered in a rash and every time Mother had to get out the zinc bath and bathe me with hot water and boracic acid powder, but I still had to do my errand and she never learned. Years later, when I reminded her of the trouble it caused, we had a good laugh about it though it wasn't funny at the time. Today we would call it an allergic reaction, I suppose.

Most of the families in Southdown and around were connected through marriage, and it used to be that one had to be careful what one said, because you could never be quite sure who you might be talking to!

I went to St John's Infant school until I was eight years old and then to the Elementary school in Victoria Road in Harpenden. Miss Davis was the much loved headmistress there and she always brought her two Highland terriers to school with her. St John's church originally stood at the corner of Crabtree Lane until it was burnt down, when a new building was erected on East Common in St John's Road in 1908. I was among the first babies to be christened there. The Rev Colley was the vicar in the early days.

He ran the Boys Brigade and they had a bugle band. We also had the St John's Girls club and we all belonged to it and loved it. It was very important to us. The Rev Colley also ran the Mothers Meeting on a Monday afternoon and my mother never missed. It used to take her two days to do the washing and ironing, but when it was Mothers Meeting she would leave it and go.

Piggotshill Lane ran up towards Wheathampstead and was bounded by six ft banks on either side and at the top, where High Firs now is, was once all fields with grazing cattle and a large pond, we used to gather wonderful mushrooms there.

The Titmus family owned the farm at the corner of St John's Road and kept cows in the meadows that stretched all along to Cravells Road. Mr Watler had his dairy by Queens Road.

I remember the forge, which stood on the site of South Harpenden Cars. Mr Rolt kept stables with ten working horses, both cart horses and dray horses and two specially for pulling the fire engine. When the fire bell rang, people rushed out to see the fire engine go tearing by pulled by these enormous creatures, it was a thrilling and very frightening sight. My brother used to wish we could have a fire at our house so that the engine could come! The stables were in Heath Road and made the road absolutely stink!

Mr Day the saddler had a thriving business in Southdown, as there were many horses then, not only working but for riding and the Herts Hunt and kennels were at Kinsbourne Green. Plenty of horses and carts about, no lorries then of course. Ogglesbys kept the forge and later used to hire out bicycles at sixpence an hour. We often had them out and often overran the time too. Later still there was a charabanc hire. People got about mostly by bike or on foot until the bus came. It was called the Cumfey Bus.

I remember the Weston family who lived in the house next to the forge. They were a family of eleven boys and one girl and they actually had a cricket team and used to play locally at Topstreet farmhouse, where the Weston-Howards lived. Christian Howard was secretary to the Bishop and lived at Hallplace Gardens in St Albans. The farmhouse is still there. I remember that none of the floors was level and there was a huge fireplace and they used to burn tree trunks on the fire, not logs but whole, supported and pushed further on as they burnt. The shepherd came every day from Mackerye End driving his flock down Crabtree Lane to the meadows below this farmhouse. When the children left school at 4.30 they would meet him and his sheep making the return journey to Mackerye End. It is nothing but houses now.

When I was little my brothers and sisters and I used to play up on the common along by Walker's Road for hours on end. In those days it was called the Prickle Dells. Often if the summer was very hot, the gorse would catch fire and burn fiercely, then summer storms would come with torrents of rain and wash the stems of the burnt gorse and we used to take the pram and break the gorse stems into manageable pieces and pile them high and take them home for kindling. They have become overgrown in recent years and now you would never know.

There used to be horse racing on Harpenden Common at the turn of the century and there was a grandstand near Limbrick Road where the club house for the golf course now stands. When I was little we used to play on the iron supports, which were all that was left. We were told not to play there but of course we did, even though we knew it was dangerous.

The family used to walk over to Hatching Green to have tea with Grandma on a Sunday afternoon and that was a great treat. I have fond memories of Childwick and walks on a Sunday evening in summer. There was a pub called the "One Bell".

There were several "characters" in Southdown. There was only one chimney sweep and his name was Jack Field and he was also a pigeon fancier. He was never out of work as everyone had coal fires then. Another was Mr Deller, the fishmonger in Cravells Road. Mr John Irons the baker, delivered his bread and wonderful home-made pork pies in a covered wooden handcart. Tramps from the workhouse in St Albans, on their way through Harpenden to Luton, were given chits to be exchanged for bread and cheese at Mr Iron's bakery, but they had to chop so much wood first.

Another character was Charlie Sibley, who owned most of the land around Southdown. He was huge, weighing between 18 and 20 stones, but he used to hunt regularly and people said he was enough to break the horse's back. He lived at The Grove, a very fine house surrounded by farm land which is still there and looking handsome though used as offices now. He is commemorated by Sibley Avenue, one of the network of roads and houses built all over his land.'

GETTING INVOLVED

'June 6th 1944. My brother, Stan Sims, brought my husband and I with our five week old baby to Westmill to escape the "doodlebugs". This previously unknown war invention had already brought down whole streets of houses around our first home in a flat in West Ham.

It was a cold day and we packed the pram with all baby's needs and just one change of clothing for us – we carried baby Janet. On arrival we were shocked to find the lady of the house was greatly displeased. She had not been consulted and naturally did not want us. Dear little Janet slept in a drawer balanced on two kitchen chairs that night. We could not return home as the last train had left. I discovered people in this wonderful beauty spot were oblivious to what was happening so near to their homes. There was only one other child in this village of elderly folk. Many generations of families had lived here – it was theirs! The Rayments, Aldridges, Pegrams etc and everyone you spoke to was a relation of someone nearby. They were kind, homely people, the baby was a great attraction and they accepted us. Because of this Stan and I vowed we would do everything we could to help the village as our "thank you". We kept that promise.

After a while my brother sold up and went to live in America. We eventually were able to rent the 17th century cottage where he had been living – 6 Pilgrims Row. We were to spend 45 years in Westmill. John our son was born after we had been in the village for four years. He and Janet both attended the excellent Westmill school. The other children all came from outlying distances and as Aspenden school had been closed, the children from there had a very long walk. The council reckoned they could manage it – poor little legs.

Very soon Stan was a busy man. He was on most of the committees and I had been persuaded to join the re-formed WI which had been put off during the war years. The WI became my whole outlet in life. My husband refused to let me go out to work and most of the village wives were in service and the men worked on the land. Mr Charles Hummerstone (who owned Pilgrims Row) had a ladder factory where there had previously been a wheelwright and a blacksmith. With the coming of cars these businesses had become redundant.

There was a lovely cottage restaurant called The 14th Century Tea Rooms, run by Mr and Mrs Bright. Eventually we had coach loads of people queuing up to go there. Tea was one shilling and threepence and included bread and butter and jam with a cake or scone and of course, a pot of tea. The dear old boy, Mr Bright, loved his olde worlde garden and made statues and pedestals for a twisted path leading to a pond with fish in it. He made a pretty bridge to stand on and roses and all old fashioned plants were in profusion.

Over the road was the village pub, The Sword in Hand, run by Mr Jackson who often appeared in a beige smock. To get beer from the barrel he trooped up and down steps to the cellar. He made and sold excellent brawn – he was famous for it. There was a scrubbed wooden counter and the wooden floorboards often had sawdust scattered around. The garden was full of trees. One day for a bet, Mr Wyant from Bury Farm walked the huge prize bull he had care of, three times around the bar – to the great astonishment of the customers. He must have found the entrance a tight fit for his "Gentle Giant".

A huge chestnut tree, considered one of the oldest in England (sadly now demolished) stood proudly by the gateway to the pub garden. In a storm in later years, a

bough overhanging the road came down and it reached the garden of the flint cottage opposite. Before it could be moved cars were driving beneath the archway it formed.

The 12th century church has not been altered externally, but the back of the altar was replaced as a gift from Mrs Murray when she came to the village. The old and very beautiful carvings that had been behind the altar were partly put on one side where Sunday school classes were held. The remainder was sold. Mrs Murray also provided the red carpeting and she herself made new kneeling mats for the altar area. Outside, the yew trees and well kept flowerbeds either side of the path made a very pretty setting for weddings. The graveyard has by now had to be extended.

Colonel MacMullen (the brewer) and his family came to live in Westmill Bury. He took charge of the Parish Council for many years, and also gave huge garden parties for his friends and employees, usually lasting three days.

One year there was enormous flooding. The water came halfway along the church wall. The sheep had been out all night and it was impossible to reach them. However, the Colonel's Spanish butler stripped off down to his long white pants and swam out to them. They followed him back to a tree at the back corner behind the church as if he was one of them. The roots had raised this old tree enough for them to crowd on and be saved. In springtime it was a wonderful sight to see when the little lambs would chase, jump and skip around.

There was a ditch running the length of the village, and often on a Sunday morning cars had to be rescued from it, especially if the grass was long. They usually belonged to pub customers. The ditch was later piped and covered over. The pump on the green remained, although it was even then not in use as water was piped mostly into gardens with a standup pipe and tap.

Half the "rec" (recreation ground) was taken over by law for the production of food during the war and we had cows or sheep on it. The rest of the area was for cricket or football. There was a play area with a strong seesaw and some other equipment. It borders the river Rib and was lovely for children to paddle or fish. Many a happy hour was spent there with a picnic.

There was a train service from Buntingford to St Margarets (all change for London or Bishops Stortford). The friendly guards would take pushchairs, prams or bikes in the guards van and the fare to Buntingford was tuppence ha'penny or threepence return. The first workmen's tickets were printed and issued to my brother whilst he was in Westmill. The driver would let anyone who wished come into his cab with him. There was a chalkpit opposite the station platform and one sad day it collapsed, and four men from Westmill died before they could be rescued. Across the main London Road another old chalkpit was cleared and on Sunday mornings men gathered there for clay pigeon shooting practice.

Every New Years Day the hunt would meet on the village green with hundreds of hounds. It was a real picture-book setting. The grass was always wet at that time of the year and the hooves ruined the green, but it was a fantastic sight when they galloped off around the bend of the road with the scarlet coated leader sounding his brass hunting horn – off to the fields and woods.

The church, school, shop, pub and tea rooms – that was the village, surrounded by old world cottages (much as it is today). The people were kind and homely and loved to keep the village looking nice. We were as one large family. The WI had renewed itself after a wartime lapse, and was interesting and popular. Menfolk had cricket, football, darts and allotments. Ladies had WI, Mother's Union, and after a while for many years, Tuesday afternoon whist. This raised money for shopping sprees and

outings. We had tradesmen calling – the butcher, baker, milkman, coalman and gipsies with pegs or lace. There was a museum, so old that it collapsed. We were using oil lamps for lighting and coal and wood for stoves and grates. Electricity came in the 1950s. You dare not wake up with a pain on a Friday morning, as the lavatory as we called it then, was at the bottom of the garden and there was a man coming to open the hatch at the back of the shed and take the bucket out! Also before daylight the man of the house would be on his way to the allotment to empty a smelly pail into a trench he had dug. Good for vegetables!

In the after war years we grew our own vegetables on allotments in the Twitchell. Most people kept chickens or rabbits, and one kept a pig. We all cooked well – proof of this was to put on weight. Wild flowers were abundant and it was a delight to take the children for a walk. We had a team of bell ringers and at Christmas handbells appeared. There were concerts and parties in the village hall, dances too but these got too crowded for the size of the hall. We also had whist drives and beetle drives.

Early in 1957, I was approached about the Best Kept Village plans. We fell for the idea as our village hall had not had repairs for 70 years. Plaster was cracking and it was looking so sad. We could get 20 points on a Village Hall. It was a wonderful village effort. Mr Hummerstone supplied materials. We made and supplied new red curtains for the stage and windows. Even ladies who employed servants came along carrying buckets and cloths, wearing overalls and headscarves. What a happy crowd we were. My family were on holiday in Minehead when a telegram came to say we had won. The Right Hon David Bowes Lyon was to come the next Saturday to present the plaque. He very kindly delayed this and when he came we had a party for all the village. Refreshments for an unknown number produced a banquet. The Ware

Town Band was placed at the top of the green and just as the ceremony was over, the heavens opened and we all crowded into the hall. We won many times after that. I am told the archives state this competition started in 1959, but we had won in 1957 and 1958.

In my old age I live in Buntingford, but memories of Westmill will remain with me for ever. The village children tying curtains around the pump for games of Mummy & Daddy; the go-carts boys made from a board on pram wheels – they would career down the road to stop at the small wall of any front garden; the naughty boys who played up Miss Chalkley, banging her gate and riding bikes into her front door; the children banging the pump handle to get Colonel Greg to come storming out – he was tall and skinny and bellowed with an unbelievable force.

Oh the memories!'

OUT IN THE COUNTRY

'There were lovely meadows, verges and ditches, and by the roadside were beautiful flowers, masses of primroses, violets, cowslips and varieties of grasses (now mostly killed by spraying). Hedgerows were a paradise for wild birds, with many pairs of yellowhammers. We used to pick strawberries, dewberries and blackberries on our way to school. Along the banks of the river Beane, kingcups, teasels and milkmaids (ladies smocks) grew and there was watercress by the ford. Trout and occasionally pike could be seen, brilliant blue kingfishers flashing overhead. In those days there was sufficient water for boys to dive from the rails on the arch behind Finchers Farm in summer, and plenty of sliding and skating in the winter.

Horses were the main strength of the farms; it was a beautiful sight to see two or three pairs of horses plodding up and down the fields ploughing. Various coloured cows grazed in the fields and milk was delivered on a float drawn by a pony, milk dipped from the churns with a measuring jug and the pony started, stopped and turned without a command. It was good to get fresh milk and eggs direct from the farms. Several farms had walnut trees, which provided a change from apple "scrumping". Beautiful barn owls, rarely seen these days, roosted in the rickyards.

In the summer holidays we took our father's tea into the harvest fields. He was the horseman at Walkern Hall and we never had to buy fruit or vegetables, as our dear father provided us with a huge vegetable and fruit garden as well as a village garden of flowers. During the war, farmers were encouraged to grow sugar beet and more grain. Many families went gleaning and some grain was kept for the hens in the backyards and some taken to Walkern mill to be exchanged for flour.

Many memories centre round Miss Georgina Cotton-Browne who owned Walkern Hall. Everyone was expected to curtsey or doff their cap when they saw her riding side-saddle on horseback or driven by her chauffeur. She was extremely generous to the village and villagers, giving Christmas parties, bringing chocolates to the school and in her will, £1 was given to each child in the village.

Ardeley and Walkern Annual Flower Show was held alternately at Walkern Hall or Ardeleybury. We entered arrangements of wild flowers.'

'My family were great walkers and like most children I was taken out every day from our farmhouse home at Ashwell. Our winter walks tended towards the hills where the roads were dry, and only in summer did we venture round Ashwell End as these roads were ankle deep in mud. Alternatively, in a dry summer we seldom saw a green hedge – they were white with dust from the roads. Today the hedges are green again, but I look with a twinge of nostalgia at dear old "Bumpety Lane" whose familiar ruts and holes lie buried under layers of tarmac.'

'Moor Green used to have two gates, one at each end and these had to be opened to let any traffic through. Because of the gates being there, cattle could graze on the green and the farms of the Green still have herbage rights, which means they are allowed to cut the green and use it for hay. We ordinary residents on the green have grazing rights. I believe I am allowed to graze some geese, a sheep and half a cow.'

'I was born in Flamstead End in 1931 and can vividly remember as a very young child playing in my grandparents' garden. My grandmother called out to me and we quickly went upstairs and saw a colourful sight of the huntsmen in their red and white outfits and black hunting caps, followed by many hounds hunting the fox. This area is now Cheshunt Golf Course.

My grandfather, Alex Clark, one of a large family born and bred in Flamstead End, owned a pony and trap. On a summer Sunday afternoon I would get a ride to Roydon, to see an uncle, who had started a nursery business in 1930, which is still being carried on by his sons. On one occasion going up Hamlet Hill, the pony stopped, unable to carry the weight of three people. Grandmother and I were told to get down from the trap and start pushing for the rest of the journey up the hill.

I can also recall grandfather selling logs and peasticks, and many times he gave gold sovereigns as change. What we would give to have a pocketful of sovereigns today.

Aunt Hilda, also one of the Clark family, would ask family and friends for help to gather the many daffodils blooming and ready for picking from the fields near Bread and Cheese Lane, Paradise. We would go around Cheshunt and neighbouring villages, laden with armfuls of daffodils for sale. Later in the year our help was again needed, to take hot drinks in enamel type billy cans with lids, together with freshly made sandwiches and home baked cakes to the haymakers.

Many older residents in the Cheshunt area will recall getting their milk, not in pint bottles, but measured in small containers from the metal churns. Ted and Kitty Judd and their milk float were a regular sight to be seen. Their brother Joe owned a pony and cart similar to my grandfather's pony and trap, and he would sell fresh fish from the cart, filleting the fish to customers' needs. I often helped by knocking on doors asking if people wanted to buy any fish, and my treat for doing this was a ride on the fishcart in Cromwell Avenue.'

THE NEW ESTATES

'When the London County Council's two estates were built in Borehamwood people fell into three categories. Not high, middle or low classes, but villagers, "outsiders", and Londoners, and it took many years for the district to be moulded into one. It seemed as if no sooner the plans were passed, than our farm land was invaded with bull-dozers carving out rough roads, and the whole area was looking devastated, as if hit by an atomic bomb, with bricks, mortar, frames, partially-built houses everywhere, and plenty of mud and puddles. The first road inhabited was Ripon Way and as soon as a house was completed a Londoner moved in.

The Church was quick to arrange for the use of a corrugated workmen's canteen for services and organisations' activities. All Saints Mission Church held its first service on the 14th October 1951. The conditions were appalling. The muddy concrete floor was cleaned, trestle tables stacked, and forms set out for worship. But the Londoners, who had sustained such heavy bombing during the war, were not going to be defeated now, and on Saturday mornings from the houses in Ripon Way came Jew and Gentile carrying mops and buckets, kneelers, books, candles, church linen and even coke for lighting and stoking the stove. With flasks of tea and coffee to fortify, they worked and chatted, getting to know each other and enjoying the company. Similarly on Sunday evenings they were back restoring the hut to a canteen.

When we had a storm the thunder reverberated throughout the nissen hut, and being on a hill, the rain poured under the corrugated sides and streamed across the floor, often to a depth of two inches. Brownie packs, Scout troop, Church Lads Brigade, Youth Club, and later a Guide Company were soon full to capacity. Whist drives, social occasions and money raising events, despite all difficulties continued to survive.

A popular figure in those days, was the priest-in-charge of All Saints Mission Church who in his raincoat, on an old motorbike, was often seen not only doing his pastoral duties, but assisting the elderly with hanging curtains, laying carpets, or moving furniture.

Local schools were full, so many children went for half a day, or to school rooms set up, such as in All Saints hall. But for many their education was at a standstill until schools could be built. The fire which gutted Furzehill School 1949/50 did not help the situation. When the new school was built it took as its emblem a phoenix rising out of the flames. In October 1953, the Mission Church moved into a small dry hut on the church site, and in September 1954 to the newly built dual-purpose hall, and was renamed "The Church of the Holy Cross".

In the village changes were rapidly taking place, the old houses where front rooms were shops disappeared, tiny terraced cottages on both sides of the road were replaced with modern shops. It was as a new arrival to Boreham Wood that I had a tooth extracted, and bleeding profusely staggered into one of these cottages to see the doctor in the back room. It was so quaint, so informal and village-like as in her front room by a roaring fire sat an old lady, who chatted so happily with all the waiting patients, that one forgot one's troubles, and was totally at ease when one saw the doctor. A similar surgery was held across the road.

The War Memorial, designed by Alan Porter and dedicated in 1922, stood at the junction of Theobald Street and Shenley Road, and on Remembrance Day the Scouts played the bugle calls. This had been instituted at the dedication, as two scouts throughout the First World War had cycled round the village blowing their bugles for the "All Clear". In about 1935, the vicar's wife Mrs Maddock, introduced the May Queen Festival to be held on Ascension Day. The Church Lads and Church Girls Brigade band led the procession of the May Queen and her retinue, flower girls, dancers and youth organisations through the village to the vicarage gardens, where the crowning ceremony took place, followed by maypole dancing and concluded with a service in church. Later the format changed and included organisations' displays, and on occasion stalls and competitions were added. Unfortunately, invariably it rained and this picturesque event had to seek shelter in the church hall.

Boreham Wood was notorious for its streams which ran from Woodcock Hill, and during heavy rain caused flooding at the Shenley Road/Furzehill Road junction. But one stream went underground and reappeared on the second LCC estate, where as a lake with ducks and wild fowl it gave great pleasure to the local residents.

The foundation stone for this area's church, St Michael's and All Angels, was laid by HRH Princess Margaret on the 23rd October 1954, the Guides and Scouts lining the route for this great occasion.

For many years visitors to Boreham Wood admired its castle on the hill. Actually this was built by MGM Studios for *Ivanhoe* but when any film required a castle this one was altered accordingly, villagers became extras, and piles of empty luncheon boxes made their appearance. When battle commenced, above the clashing of armour and yells, the Producer's voice resounded shouting instructions.

After the war, All Saints church had a farthing fund, and with other amounts collected, built an addition to the church – a Thanksgiving Tower which opened in 1957 and became famous throughout the world for its 72 minutes to the hour clock. Fame quickly died when the clock face was eventually altered.

So Boreham Wood became a town, and in doing so lost its ancient name – Boreham Wood was made one word. Easier to put on signs and buses someone declared!'

'For a few years, my husband and two children lived with my mother, then we moved to a small cottage in Hertford, two up and two down – toilet across the yard, no hot water and only gas lighting, but it was a home of our own.

In 1953, we were lucky enough to move in to a brand new house on Sele Farm Estate. We now had three children and at that time my husband (now a teacher) was recalled to the Navy for the Korean emergency. Although we were lucky to have a new house, life on the estate was real pioneering. We had no shops, schools, street lights, buses and no made up footpaths. Every morning I had to take my seven year old daughter and three year old and eight month old sons down to Hertford North station and put her on the bus to go to school in Hertford. Fortunately this didn't last long, she changed schools and went to Port Vale where she could walk with others from the estate.'

OLD CHARACTERS

'I do not doubt that the characters one knew in childhood had a greater impact on one's thoughts, and were more memorable than those one met in later life. They certainly seemed more colourful.

Bill I encountered almost daily when he worked as a general hand for a smallholder in our neighbourhood. His greeting, "'Ow dew, Miss" never varied, and always a kindly smile wreathed his expressive weather-beaten face which had mellowed like medieval vellum. He moved with a heavy methodic plod come rain or shine, and the cows which he guided to and from the grazing meadows appeared to adjust to his lethargic walk, swishing their tails in agreement as they pursued their leisurely way. Nevertheless, I could not decide whether it was Bill or the cattle which dictated the languorous procession. Bill always carried a hefty knot-topped stick, but never did I see this used other than in support of his person.

Jack was an entirely different personality from Bill. I allude to him so with diffidence, as someone with such a one-track mind cannot truthfully be so described. I was always fearful of meeting him face-to-face when I heard he was frequenting the neighbourhood, as his approach was usually heralded by inebriated and incoherent utterings which rang distantly in the clear country air. His cavortings and his rantings were usually enlivened by a few choice expletives. Jack sought casual employment as he traversed the countryside, but his chances of obtaining seasonal work were diminished by such shenanigans and acerbity.

I am unable to recall my first meeting with George. I knew simply that he existed, and that we were bound to meet periodically. George unfortunately entered this world deprived of the ability of hearing and speech, but due to his parents' dedication and a little schooling, this deaf-mute was eventually able to communicate in an abstract manner. After his parents demise he continued to live in the cottage of his birth, but this was eventually razed to the ground by fire. Fortunately George escaped uninjured, and it was then that he became a gentleman-of-the-road. He was rubicund, whiskered, white-bearded and elderly when I first noticed his visits to our village. He tended to shuffle along with the aid of a long staff, and it was most eerie when walking along a country road at night, suddenly to become aware of this sinister and ghostly shuffle.

George's family were known to my mother in her youth when she lived at a nearby farm, and doubtless the remembrance was reciprocal as George would occasionally call on us hoping that a meal may be forthcoming. Many a hot dinner, or a plate of hot buttered toast, cake and tea, depending upon the time of day, was provided to gladden his heart. He was truly grateful.

George had a most amiable approach, and one enjoyed the feeling of warmth and sincerity conveyed by his memorable smile which lightened his kindly blue eyes. His benevolent mien belied the fact that he owned nothing tangible with which to be charitable. He was a man of courage, and I am glad to have known him.'

DOWN THE VILLAGE STREET

What village would be without its pub and its little shop? Sadly all too many have disappeared over the last few years, but memory recalls the 'old boys' sitting round the fire smoking their clay pipes, and the rare treat of home-made ice cream. And if you thought that the lamplighter was a character out of a Dickens' novel, think again!

THE PUB

'The "Shoulder of Mutton" in Pirton was a very old pub and this is where I was brought up. There were nine really regular customers and they never varied in their habits; all sat in their own place on the bench or chair. I could tell where they were and what they would be doing any time of the day. They didn't know what dishonesty was; if they were playing dominoes with my father, one might just get up, go and help himself to beer and say "I've put the money in the box, Charles."

Beer and tobacco were kept in the cellar and they would help themselves to tobacco too. It was in half ounce packets, Light Oak, Dark British Oak and Gold Flake cigarettes also Woodbines – five in a packet! That was our stock.

The brewers used to supply clay pipes free of charge. All the old boys used to have a clay pipe. They would break the stem off until the bowl was just a little longer than their nose. First they would measure them and mark round until they could snap the stem and after smoothing the mouthpiece off to their satisfaction, they would make two little grooves in it and wind some cotton round so that it wouldn't slip out of their mouths. Before they filled the new pipe they would drop it into their beer to soak; they reckoned it made the baccy taste sweeter.

On Sundays whoever was sitting by the fire would look after our joint and baste it. The gravy wasn't made with powder like today, they would get a spoonful of sugar and put it in the embers, after a few seconds it would go brown and then burst into flames and sizzle up, then it was stirred into the fat.

When I was about 17 years old, the thatch caught fire and as the only water came from the village pond, when at last the fire engine came all the way from Hitchin and put the hose in the pond, it clogged up with weeds and mud and stopped working. People did try to throw buckets of water about, but it burned down quickly and now there is no trace of it.'

'The two pubs at Burnham Green in the 1920s were very popular. The White Horse had a skittle alley. The Duck was kept by old Mr Burrows and his two bachelor sons, Ernie and Freddie. They sold sweets at the back door – vinegar flaps, sherbet fountains and packets of chocolate coconut tobacco, all for a halfpenny.'

'My uncle was the landlord of the Long and Short Arm at Lemsford. When he decided to give it up he asked my father if he would like to take over, so we moved to Lemsford village where I helped my father in the day-to-day running of the pub; those were the days when one arrowroot biscuit was a penny and a pint of mild beer and five Woodbine cigarettes were fourpence each.

When the war started soldiers arrived at the pub and took over the lounge for working purposes as there was an Italian prisoner of war camp in the village. When the bombing started my mother suggested we take our beds down into the cellar. My father moved the barrels to allow space for the beds, as it had two ways to get out if one outlet became blocked. I think the smell of the beer barrels helped us to sleep.

There were a lot of soldiers stationed in Welwyn Garden City and they used to come down and spend the evening in the pub, which is how I met my husband. We were married at Lemsford church in 1943 and had a lovely wedding reception in the pub, most of the entertainment done by the soldiers stationed in the village.

My mother suffered from rheumatism and after a while she became worse and was unable to carry on helping my father so we moved into a house in the village owned by Mr Wackett, who took over as landlord of the pub, and where my first daughter was born in 1945, just as the last "doodlebug" was going over this area.'

THE SHOP

'Our village shop and post office at Little Munden was small then, in the early years of the century, but everybody knew everybody else and it was certainly a meeting place. Nobody was collecting pensions – there was no such thing in those days. No tinned soup or fruit either, but biscuits, flour, and dried fruit which had to be weighed and placed in blue sugar paper bags. Sweets were put up in a screwed-up cone of newspaper twisted at the top and the bottom.

The smell of cheese-bacon-paraffin seemed to blend together. There was tobacco, Wills Woodbine cigarettes at twopence for ten, laces, candles, flypapers and lamp wicks, ribbons, cottons and lace – you name it and it was to be found there.'

'Our sweet shop at Welwyn was really just a room in a house, with the counter on one side against the wall and there were tables and chairs spread about, as they also sold cups of tea. The cycling clubs from London stopped here on their way to Bedford and beyond and again on the way back. It was a little gold mine especially at the weekends. These cyclists dressed for the part, long socks to the knees and narrow breeches with little lightweight shoes and for wet weather yellow oilskins with leggings, cape and sou'wester, and rode real racing bikes of the time. They rode in blocks of 20 or more sometimes. They went so fast it was hard to count them. At bluebell time

Pubs, cafes and tea gardens made a living catering for the cyclists' clubs which were so popular before the Second World War.

one could see them returning home with huge bunches strapped to the back of their saddle bags.

At the sweet shop one could buy boiled sweets four ounces for twopence. All I had to spend at one time was a half penny.'

'As a child my parents kept a small village grocer's shop in Standon with a green at the front with railings around. This was the hub of village life especially on a Sunday. I was about ten years old at the time (1937 or so).

On a Friday we would have a lorry turn up dripping water in a trail all the way up the road. On this lorry would be huge blocks of ice. I would watch these large blocks off-loaded into a hole filled with clean sacks and carefully covered up.

My father was a very enterprising man, hoping to make a little extra money. On a Saturday night, he would boil up milk to add to ice-cream powder, more like custard I should imagine, and early Sunday morning father would be breaking up ice and with freezing salt packing it round a drum which was fitted into a wooden tub, with a fixed handle on top. We had to take turns winding the handle (to make the middle drum spin) for about half an hour, but at the end of it there was the most beautiful ice-cream which we sold on our front green on trestle tables.

The local children came from all around, as it was a rare taste in those days. One penny cornets, twopenny wafers. Also lots of cycle clubs used to be around, coming from as far as Waltham Abbey and Dagenham. More so when they discovered it was a good watering hole with ice cream, Tizer and lemonade. Then my father branched out selling teas and cakes in a little side room, and we were kept busy all day with me helping in all ways I could – at the end of the day, heaven, we were allowed to finish up the ice cream in the tub!

We used to watch the water-cart going down to the river. The horse would go into the ford and have a lovely cool paddle, while his driver would scoop the water into a container to take back to the farm for the cows to drink when they were in the milking shed.

In those days the milk would be delivered by horse and cart with a big churn on board, and the milkman would knock on the door and fill your jugs from the measures hung on the side of his large can. It was so rich we used to leave it in bowls to settle and skim off the cream and put it in a screw-top jar, shake it for a while and hey-presto – butter! A little extra was a treat during the war years.'

LIGHTS AND DUSTCARTS

'At Redbourn between the wars, the lamplighter made his round on bicycle, balancing a long pole as he rode – one tug with his pole at each lamp standard and the light appeared. Gas was supplied to some houses but often only downstairs, so candles were used at bedtime. Fragile gas mantles were always handled with great care.'

'In Berkhamsted in the 1930s and 1940s the dustcart was pulled by a shire horse with huge feet. The cart had two large lids on the pavement side which were opened by putting a foot on a long low bar – then the lid flew up and the dustman hurled the contents of the bin on his back into the cart.'

CHURCH AND CHAPEL

Sunday was a special day, when little, if any, work was done and the family often attended church twice a day. For the children it meant Sunday school – and the much looked forward to Sunday school outing or treat.

SUNDAY WAS A SPECIAL DAY

'Sundays at home were strictly observed. My dad was a churchman and sang in the Walkern church choir. He did not believe in any kind of enjoyment or work on the Sabbath. He did not shave, nor did he allow even the cleaning or polishing of shoes – they had to be done on the Saturday before. He always wore his best suit to church. If my sisters or I wanted to do a bit of knitting or sewing of a Sunday afternoon, we had to sit behind Father's chair in the parlour and take the risk!

In the spring we had the pleasure of picking 24 daffodils and snowdrops from the rectory garden – no doubt to stop them being picked without permission.'

'There was chapel to attend on Sunday mornings, always wearing best clothes. A new spring coat for Easter and a new dress and straw hat for White Sunday. During my early years, sport on Sunday was almost non-existent. As recreation I was taken on long walks and learned about wild flowers and discovered birds nests, which were on no account to be plundered. On Sunday evenings the family gathered around the piano for a sing song.'

'I was born in Colney Heath and was the youngest of eight children. My father was the manager of the nearby waterworks.

We lived a very plain and simple diet, but the highlight of the week was Sunday afternoon when Tommy Lipton (Sir Thomas Lipton) used to come to Colney Heath and stop near the church and hand out boxes of chocolates to all the children.

We used to climb all over the car and when the chauffeur tried to push us away, he was rebuked by Sir Thomas with "Leave the children alone." In the winter he used to bring us nice gloves – astrakhan with leather palms.

He drove in a gleaming black car with enormous polished brass head lamps. He had the hood down always even if it was raining. Sometimes he would bring very smartly dressed ladies with him and they used to help distribute the chocolates. (No wonder the chauffeur was cross when we climbed all over the car in our muddy boots.) When he left Colney Heath he went to a little village called Coopers Green and did the same to the children there.

What a grand old man he was – shame he didn't win the America Cup in Shamrock!'

'As young kids we were made to go to Sunday school mornings and afternoons; we would go for a walk afterwards and my husband remembers having to take his invalid cousin in his bath-chair with them when he and his brothers went out. They would take him along a brook which is on the boundary of Waltham Cross and Enfield and push him down the slopes of the brook, through the water and up the other side! Great fun!'

GOING TO CHURCH

'My family were very strict members of the church and Sundays were days which consisted of Sunday school at ten o'clock and afterwards into church for matins. We then went home for dinner, with another session of Sunday school in the afternoon at three. If there was a baptismal service afterwards we would watch that. Usually we went to tea with my grandparents, most of the relatives gathered there on Sundays and after tea it was often into church again for evensong. We didn't get much opportunity to play on a Sunday.

Good Friday and Easter Monday were days when we would walk across the fields from Bishops Stortford to Thorley Wood to gather primroses and violets.'

'A Methodist chapel had been built right onto the village shop at Ayot in mid-Victorian times which still had a thriving congregation of about 60 people well into this century – now both are desirable residences.

The chapel did not detract from the congregation at Ayot St Peter (built in 1875). Every Sunday the two Misses Wilshere, the last survivors of that family, drove in stately carriage progress to church on a track over their own land and past their West Lodge with a large wayside plaque commemorating the family mounted on the wall, followed by their farmworkers on foot. Garden parties were held at the old rectory, when even the citizens of Ayot St Lawrence put in an appearance. The Wilshere Estate has been broken up, there are still some working farms, but house and park now belong to Smith, Kline and Beecham.'

'The church had a much greater influence on family life in the past. Dad was a sidesman and we lived next door to the church so we had no option! Two services a day were held in Bayford church, and the choir was a large one. Everyone went to church and usually to both services. New mothers were expected to go to church for thanksgiving of a safe delivery of a new baby. The choir children all enjoyed the annual party in the village hall and especially the coach trip to Clacton – many children didn't see the sea till they were ten or eleven years old.'

'A Baptist chapel (long since gone) was one of the places at Burnham Green that the children went to Sunday school. There was also a small Church of England church but though this building still stands it is no longer a church. I went to both Sunday schools during my childhood. At the Baptist chapel we had lovely seaside outings. At the church on Mothering Sunday we were given small bunches of flowers to take home to our mum; they would consist of violets, snowdrops and primroses. This little church had an organ and someone had to stand by the organist and pump a large handle up and down.'

'When I was young in about 1931, less than five years old, I attended church with my grandparents. We started from their house together, but at the top of the hill we three stopped. My grandparents looked at me and asked which one I wished to go with, for one was Methodist and the other Baptist, and all their lives attended separate establishments in the same town. I always stood very still and listened intently, not to their question but to the rustle of papers. For my grand-dad always put sweets in his pocket, but grandma put chocolate bars in hers. If I felt like sweets I went with grand-dad and as I mostly did prefer sweets, I became a life long Methodist. It was a sweet way to Heaven!'

'My father was the verger of the church at Aldbury for 25 years, as well as the local gravedigger. It was in the days when there was no electricity, so the church, like people's homes, used paraffin oil lamps. Heating for the church was by coke-filled furnace. Electricity was eventually installed in 1929.

Surviving from the generosity of benevolent people in the 17th century, there was a "Bread Charity" from which the deserving poor persons who attended church were given a loaf of bread – but when it was discovered that children were paid a penny to collect it and that it was being used to feed their pets, this charity was discontinued.

'Just after the war, everything at Clothall seemed to revolve around the lead on the church roof. Half of it was stolen and we buckled to with appeals, garden parties, whist drives and plain hard work to buy copper for a new roof. Then some of the remaining lead went and it started all over again. Now we have a complete copper roof which makes a noise like a percussion instrument on windy days.

Before the war at Baldock, the "curfew" was still rung once a week.'

SUNDAY SCHOOL

'I was born in Walkern in a house on the High Street. This village is east of Stevenage and yet very rural. The first thing I can really remember was going to Sunday school at the Old Rectory at the time of the then rector the Rev Gibbs and Mrs Gibbs. The Old Rectory is now a private residence and the Long Room is still as large as it was then and adjoining the main house. We had lessons in the Long Room – oh! it was so big to a little girl. We had this before the eleven o'clock service and if we wanted to we went over the bridge with the weir under, as there was so much water running over it – to this service of matins. The present bridge is by the ford and the river Beane is very low and the scene changed.

Sunday school was very enjoyable. One thing sticks in my mind. At Christmas time we made "cribs" from half a walnut shell with a clove for the baby Jesus and cotton wool for covers. There was a Christmas party in the village hall and chocolates were thrown amongst us by Miss Cotton-Browne (sometime churchwarden and patron of the village) and we grabbed as many as possible. Each Sunday we collected a text to stick on our cards for attendance and those with the most were presented with prizes.'

'We attended Walsworth Road Baptist church when we were young and it was usual to walk to church and back for morning and evening service plus Sunday school in the afternoon. When it was Sunday School Anniversary we girls always had a new dress and hat and wore a buttonhole of lilies of the valley picked from the garden.'

'When a small child in the late 1920s I lived with my parents at Hatfield, and on most Sundays, high days and holidays Miss White, a friend of my parents, came to lunch. She was a short and roundish lady who always wore unrelieved black from top to toe – this puzzled me for her name was White. Her cheeks were like rosy apples, a pince-nez sat on her nose, her grey hair formed a bun on top of her head, and a black tricorn hat sat on top of the bun. This hat and her black calf-length cloak were worn all year, only the voluminous clothes underneath changing with the seasons – these reached her toes and had many pockets, for no bag was ever carried but only a big black umbrella.

Miss White appreciated my mother's cooking and when it was a "roast beef day" I watched with glee for her first taste of horseradish sauce (Mother scraped her own and it was very strong) and waited for the tears that rolled down her rosy cheeks, to be mopped up with a large white handkerchief. When the moment came to choose her "sweet" she always said "A little of everything please". (I tried the same idea, but it didn't work for me!) After lunch she would grab me firmly by the hand and take me unwillingly to Sunday school, where she was a teacher.'

'My father, a kind but serious man, was superintendent of a large Sunday school in Islington and in 1920, when I was five years old I was allowed for the first time to join mother and older sister on the annual Sunday school treat that he had arranged for the whole school, boys, girls and infants.

About 150 excited children boarded a specially designated steam train at Highbury station one summer Saturday morning, and enjoyed the all too brief journey to the tiny station at Bricket Wood where Gray's Fair awaited them and fun was to be had in the woods.

When the train arrived at the station, the children and teachers quickly alighted happy in their expectation of the pleasures to come, and flocked bubbling with excitement to the fair ground. However while they went on their way, my mother drew my sister and me aside, engaged a pony and trap and after helping us safely aboard asked for us all to be taken to St Albans.

It was the first time I had ever had such a ride and the

56

rhythmic trotting of the pony delighted me, so too did the feel of the breeze in my hair, but I was absolutely amazed and enchanted by the colourful hedgerows and the grass verges dotted with so many flowers (all vivid hues) which I could not name. I gazed entranced at the sight. So many lovely flowers growing so freely were a revelation to a town child. I expect that when we reached St Albans Abbey (did the trap really clatter into Sumpter Yard or did I dream it?) my mother arranged for us to be guided round the building, if so, I remember nothing of it, but when we were on the point of leaving by the south transept door, my attention was called to the painting of *The Passing of Queen Eleanor* by Frank Salisbury.

Whether I was touched by the story of King Edward I's devotion to his Queen as he followed the cortege to London, or whether it was the picture itself alive with the light of the torches heightening the brightly coloured robes of the escorts while the sorrowing King followed in the shadow, I do not know. But I was deeply impressed and thought about the story and the picture all the way back to Bricket Wood.

When we rejoined my father we had tea, but I remember little about it except there was an abundance of watercress and that somehow I managed to get blackcurrant stains on my dress to my mother's annoyance!

Later as the children assembled for the return journey, many carried souvenirs for their parents while others held bunches of garden flowers bought at the gates of cottages for a few pence, but I was too absorbed by my experiences of the day to be envious of them for I had memories of the wild flowers in the lanes of Bricket Wood and the picture of *The Passing of Queen Eleanor* to take with me into the future. (The picture was removed from the Abbey by thieves who cut it out of its frame. It has never been located. I believe this happened sometime after the Second World War.)'

'Sunday school treats were held at Broxbournebury with games and food in the grounds. It was while in Sunday school that the first aeroplane ever to be seen in Broxbourne flew over. We all rushed out to see and witnessed the pilot bailing out into a tree while his plane ignominiously crashed.'

'I discovered the joy of Sunday school at St Etheldreda's church up the steep hill near the gatehouse of the Hatfield House estate. My friends and I usually had a penny to put in the plate, but I'm afraid sin overtook us on the way, for we took time to pop into "Topsy Wigley's" little sweet shop and spend a halfpence, leaving a halfpence for the plate!'

'We attended the Methodist Sunday school at Walkern, twice on Sundays, and treats were held in the Manor Farm barn. A friend remembers how most children saw Hovis bread only on these occasions and it was always the first to go. The annual summer outing was to Clacton. At one time there were five places of worship in the village – the parish church, Wesleyan, Congregational, Strict Baptist and Mission Hall.'

'The highlight of the year for Redbourn children was the United Sunday Schools annual outing, when a special train was chartered to take children and parents to Southend on Sea. Schools closed for the day and the village was deserted. When the weary travellers returned, many of them had a long walk home but everyone was used to walking then.'

'I was born in Northchurch in 1932 and we lived in the High Street for 18 months. My mother was asked by the neighbours if she would refrain from drying nappies outside on the Sabbath.

In 1937 aged five, I attended Sunday school at St Peter's church, Berkhamsted. I had twopence to put in the collection – as did my friends. We only ever put one penny in and the other would buy four gobstoppers or two bubblegums or "Spanish Wood" (a chewy liquorice stick) at Bunyan's sweetshop (where Waitrose is now). In 1940, a Sunday School teaparty was given by the teacher at her home. With the tea a small pot of "pills" appeared on the table. "What are those?" said I. My friend replied, "That's saccharine instead of sugar." I had never seen it before so I put a teaspoonful in my tea!'

HOUSE & HOME

HOW WE LIVED THEN

◝

No electric light, no heating except the coal fire or the kitchen range, no running water, no indoor toilets – life was lived without mod cons even into fairly recent times. Seeing the 'desirable residences' of some of today's villages, it is as well to remember that only modern services have made them warm and comfortable. It was very different for their original occupants, as many people remember.

NO MOD CONS

'We had no electricity, we had no piped water. My parents, my two younger brothers and my father's brother and I, lived on a small mixed farm of just under 100 acres in the parish of Redbourn in the 1910s and 1920s.

The only transport for the family was one push bike on which my father would go to the St Albans market once a week. The rest of the family walked, to Flamstead to church and to Redbourn for shopping.

We kept four horses, two cows to provide milk for the house and to suckle a couple of calves, and various sows and pigs and some store cattle. The chickens had a large stone barn for their nest boxes and perches and were free to range over the farmyard and rickyard as they pleased.

We had a deep well for drinking water and my father let down a large bucket on a strong rope and wound it up as in the old traditional (Jack and Jill) wells. The cover was kept locked as the well was very deep and went right down into the chalk. For washing and cleaning we used rain water which was pumped up into the kitchen from an underground cistern into which water from the roofs drained. The animals drank from a pond near the farmyard and when this sometimes went dry we had to take a watercart to Redbournbury Mill to get water from the river Ver.

Indoors our kitchen was furnished with a stove with an open fire, an oven on one side and a small tank for hot water on the other. In the mornings my father lit the fire and put a kettle on to boil for breakfast before going out to feed the animals. In one corner of the kitchen was a large copper with space for a fire underneath, this was lit on Monday mornings and then filled with water from the pump for the week's washing. We had a large cool pantry facing north where food could be stored. Our groceries and bread were delivered by pony trap from Redbourn, and the grocer returned with boxes of eggs. We had to go to the village for our meat.'

'Belsize was a very small, intimate community in the 1920s, with a row of cottages, a pub and a couple of farms. Of course there was no running water, electricity, gas or mains drainage, until at least the 1950s. Water was from the well, one shared between three or four cottages. What a great day when one cold water tap was installed under the archway to serve the whole row, which was "one-up" on Sarratt, which relied for much of its water on a pump on the green, now preserved. Oil lamps and candles lit the room, oil stoves and blackleaded ranges were for cooking – the best rice pudding came from the little oven next to the fire. An innovation was the tinbox which stood on top of the oil stove – a handy oven, especially in summer.

Washing day meant that the big copper which was built into the scullery had a fire lit underneath it, and in went the clothes for a good boil. The various flat irons were heated up in readiness by the fire. The copper was also lit for bath nights, the scullery being warm and cosy, with the hip-bath in the middle of the floor.

Of course, there was no mains drainage, the privy in the backyard had lilac and mock orange growing over it as an early deodorant! My dad always had a trench dug across the vegetable plot, in which vegetable peelings, washing up water etc were put. When the trench was full, it was filled in and another dug, hence huge vegetables were grown from all the watering and manuring. Huge red gooseberries, filbert nuts and hundreds of snowdrops in rich black soil are favourite memories.'

'I was born in the early 1920s at Burnham Green. My father was born in this village, Datchworth parish, as were his parents before him. The village belonged to four parishes, Welwyn, Digswell, Tewin and Datchworth. We lived in a tied cottage, as my grandfather was a gardener for Lord Cowper at Panshanger House. My paternal grandparents died during the Great War and my father, being the youngest of 13 children, returned to the house when he returned from the war and married my mother. There were outhouses at the bottom of the garden where the washing was done, also the "toilet" was in one of them. We kept pigs and chickens also.

In 1927 we moved across the road to the new council houses, now in Welwyn parish where there was cold running water and a bath. Before this water was fetched from the water pump outside a row of farmhouses. It had a large lion head and a handle was pumped up and down until the water came from the lion's mouth. In frosty weather a fire was lit, usually of newspaper, to thaw the tap. A big brick copper was in the bathroom and the fire had to be lit to heat the water, which had to be bucketed from the bath for the washing and for our baths. Friday night only in those days, which was also the time we all lined up, seven of us, for our weekly dose of liquorice powder.

Only the wealthy could afford the new labour-saving devices, such as this early vacuum cleaner.

The new house had a large garden which my father ("me Dad") cultivated. He was a keen vegetable grower. When the potatoes were harvested, he clamped them all, a large mound of earth covered them, and they were dug out as and when needed, a bit difficult in frosty weather.

We had a large barn at the bottom of the garden with a chicken house and run attached. Today it would be called a large garden shed, but no-one called them sheds, always a barn.

The house had gas lighting and we had a gas cooker with a penny meter, but most of the cooking was done on a coal fire range in the living room, which had an oven. I, being the eldest girl, had to blacklead the grate with "Zebra" blacklead, and the steel on the stove had to be cleaned with emery paper, or with a wet cloth dipped in the ashes. The steel fender was also cleaned this way. The gas mantles were fragile and always seemed to be disintegrating. Electricity came much later.

The women of the village used to go "wooding". I used to go with an aunt. We walked to the woods and gathered up the old fallen wood. Long bundles were made, then tied up with string or rope. The bundles were carried home on our head, we put an old cushion or a pad on our head first. This wood was mainly used for the copper to heat the water. Looking back, and at the same time thinking of the antiques business today, I dread to think what was "shoved up the copperhole".'

'Now a conservation area with "desirable residences", life in the Ayots was very different in the 1920s and 1930s when cottages had neither water nor electricity, only outside sanitation and most residents drew their water from a pump on the village green – some not only for their own use but also to earn a few pence taking it in buckets to the larger cottages. Buckets were repeatedly repaired with metal bungs when they sprang a leak, a new bucket being a major expense. Jonnie Field from St Albans, who only died recently, came once a week to deliver paraffin for oil lamps, candles, new buckets etc. Bath water had to be heated in the copper in the outside washhouse.

There were some exceptions to this. The then Lord Brocket built some houses in about 1921 which actually won the *Daily Mail* award for the best labourers' cottages of the year because they had inside water and loos. By about 1940, Captain Wilshere of the Frythe – a big local landowner – prevailed upon the rural District Council to have water and electricity supplies to the Ayots.'

'My parents, and their children, moved from Tottenham to Waterford in 1937 (as a result of the depression). We lived in a small cottage in which my grandparents had previously lived. There was no hot water, no bathroom and no sanitation. Our lavatory was in a wooden hut down the garden (very dark and spooky to a small child) which was emptied by my father each week into a very large hole at the bottom of the garden. Toilet paper was newspaper cut into squares and kept on a meat skewer! Bathtime took place once a week in the scullery in a long tin "bungalow" bath. The water was heated in an electric copper – youngest child first and my dad in last! Hair-washing took place once a fortnight at the scullery sink.

My sister and I had to sleep together in a small double bed (which caused many squabbles) and my dad would bring us a saucepan of hot water each morning so that we could wash. The winters seemed much colder in those days – the windows always had "Jack Frost" all over them. The kitchen was the only room heated (by a black-leaded kitchen range on which Mum did a lot of the cooking) and therefore was the room constantly in use. The "front room" was only for high days and holidays.'

'It was an unforgettable thrill switching on the newly-installed electric light in our cottage at Westmill in 1947 – but how over-bright the rooms felt without the oil lamps' warm glow.

Paths outside the cottages were made from the ashes of the fires in the grates and there was a special crunchiness to walking on them.'

'There was no gas or electric in the house we moved into in Digswell in 1945, we had to use oil lamps for light and had a kitchen range and primus stove for cooking. Candles were used for light in the bedrooms. There was one water tap between two houses, and no hot water except what was boiled in a copper in the shed. The earth toilet was round the back. The rent for this property was five shillings a week.'

'At the end of the war Mrs Day was married but had been living with her sister in Roehampton while her husband had been in the RAF. When he was demobbed they wished to return to Offley, his home village, but there was nowhere to live. His mother and father already had three grown up sons living at home. Finally an old lady offered Mr Day a couple of rooms in her council house and he jumped at the chance.

They had a living room, a bedroom, a shared kitchen, a toilet just outside the back door and a good sized garden for growing vegetables. In the kitchen, the cooking was done on a coal fired range and all the hot water had to be heated by lighting the fire under the copper. This caused dust and soot and the flue had to be cleaned out every two weeks. This meant climbing up on a chair and raking out the soot. However hard she tried, Mrs Day always managed to get black-bright by the time she had finished. She hated it, so it was not surprising that when she and her husband took over the tenancy, the first thing they did was to get the council to take out the kitchen range, the range in the front room and the copper and replace them all with electric. The only trouble then was, when the meters were fitted, they were fixed so high up the wall, Mrs Day had to climb up on a chair to put the money into them!

It was not until 1950 that a bath was put in by the council – but it had no running water, that was not available until 1975. When Mrs Day worked at Offley Place as a housemaid in the late 1930s all the laundry was sent out, now she had to do everything by hand, the only help being a large wooden mangle. The terry nappies had to be boiled, washed, mangled, hung out to dry and then aired over the clothes horse in front of the fire.

There were a couple of shops in the village, plus the post office and the butcher's. The baker called in his van twice a week, but most of the shopping was done either in Luton or Hitchin. The grocers would deliver but Mrs Day preferred to get her Co-op "divi" and carry her goods home on the bus, the fare being a shilling return.'

'We came to live in Little Gaddesden in 1949. We travelled up in the removal van, my two little boys and I, sitting on two armchairs amidst the rest of the furniture. We arrived at Little Gaddesden House about four o'clock. It was dark, cold, wet and really miserable. My husband had not yet returned from the school where he was teaching, but the housekeeper showed us into the rooms that were to be our home for the next three months. We lived in the kitchen, as our lounge was up a passage, across the hall – and as coal was still rationed and we had not yet registered we could not light a fire there in any case. The cost of heating the room was beyond our meagre means. Our two bedrooms were again along the passage and up the grand staircase, very lofty and of course very cold, as was the barn-like bathroom.

But the morning after our arrival was bright and sunny and my husband took us to see the Golden Valley. As we walked down the Black Path, the beauty of the valley and Ashridge Park hit us. At that time the park was covered in bracken and brambles and many more trees, which still had their leaves although they had changed to their autumn tints. The mist rising from the wet ground was shot through with sunlight, it was truly a Golden Valley.'

AT THE END OF THE GARDEN

'My family lived in Southdown, Harpenden in the 1910s; there were nine children including myself. Sanitation at our house in Cravells Road was poor to begin with. The toilet was an earth closet across the garden and Father had the unenviable job of emptying it. Later things were better and we were connected to the main sewerage system, but we still had an outside toilet.'

'In the 1920s we were still having to make do with outside closets in Shenley. The containers in these closets were collected and emptied each Friday evening by two men with a cart. There was a story that did the rounds about these men. It was said that on one occasion one of them dropped his coat into the contents of the cart. He started fishing around for it and his mate said, "You're not going to get it out again are you?" to which he replied, "'Course I am, my sandwiches are in the pocket!".'

'I was brought up at Lye Lane, Bricket Wood and my grandparents were coal merchants and contractors. They used horses and carts 60 years ago, when coal was one shilling and tenpence a hundredweight. There was a special round metal cart that was not allowed to go out before ten o'clock at night and was used for emptying toilets round the villages. My grandmother would prepare the lanterns for it.'

'In the great houses at Aldbury – Stocks, Brightwood, Toms Hill House, the Old Rectory in what was then called The Holloway – even into the 1930s, only the gentry had WCs. The butlers, housemaids and cooks had to use earth closets and they had to go across the yard to reach them. The contents were then buried in the garden. In winter weather this could be very trying.'

FETCHING THE WATER

⊸

Every drop of water had to be fetched into the house, whether from a communal tap, a pump or a well on the village green. Washday was already drudgery enough without the effort required to fill the copper – the soaking, boiling, washing, rinsing, blueing, mangling and drying taking up the whole of Monday. Bathnight too was something of a chore, and one bath had to do for several people – cleanest first! For some people, the public slipper baths had to take the place of today's private bathrooms.

PUMPS AND WELLS

'I was born in 1903 in Little Munden. The village midwife from the next hamlet was called upon to bring me into the world in our "two up, two down" cottage, plus a lean to scullery. No running water but three tall barrels at the back door to catch rainwater. Drinking water was carried from the 160ft well at the end of the lane, using a yoke over the shoulders to keep the pails steady and so save spillage.'

'Near the Men's Institute on the grass at Welham Green was the village pump, where the menfolk came with their yokes to carry two buckets of water home. I used to love sitting in my hip bath in front of a lovely fire in the kitchen range, having my bath.'

'Water at Sarratt Bottom came from a well in the garden, which dried up when the water level fell as the pumping station for mains water was opened further along the valley.'

'Years ago before the days of tapped water in the home, there were in the village of Hinxworth, north Hertford-shire, several deep wells, where the villagers would get their water by bucket for use in the home. One of these wells, situated in the High Street, had a pump attachment but unfortunately the well became polluted and was put out of use. The Parish Councillors of the day were asked in vain to put the matter right. But as of today the wheels of officialdom moved very slowly, despite the pleadings of those who had to walk some distance to the school house to get water. For fun some of the village girls decided to dress the pump up, as it was no use for anything else. This they did and named it "Dorcas". The next day they discovered that overnight a poem had been written and tied to the pump – it read –

> A few more years shall roll
> A few more rates to pay
> And we shall carry water
> From the school house day by day
> Oh, Parish Councillors
> Prepare your souls for this great day
> When we shall have enough water
> To wash your sins away.

No-one really knew who wrote the poem, but several had a good idea.'

WASHDAY AND BATHNIGHT

'Water was obtained from wells or pumps strategically placed round Redbourn village. Monday was always washday when the copper was filled with cold water and the fire lit underneath. While the water was heating, clothes were scrubbed by hand and put into the copper to boil. Hours later they were taken out, rinsed in a zinc bath and then mangled. They were then dipped in "blue" water for final rinsing and mangled again. Collars, table-cloths and aprons were stiffened by being dipped into Robin starch. Finally everything was pegged on clothes lines which were permanent features of every garden. Some housewives had their clothes lines on the common where they always caught the breeze. Ironing was done with flat irons heated on the fire – spit to see if they are hot enough! A woman could earn half a crown by doing the family washing and ironing. The zinc wash tub was used again on Fridays for the family bath. Water was heated in the copper and carried in buckets to the tub placed by the fire.'

'When I was first married, the copper for washing clothes was in the bathroom but there was no water laid on. It took about seven trips to the pump to fill the copper. Then a fire was lit underneath to boil the water. The washing was rubbed on a washboard. Rinsing involved more trips for water and finally an old mangle squeezed out as much water as possible. In this way washing took all day.'

'In our Barnet house the copper was heated by gas. The family mangle with its wooden rollers was passed on in the 1950s to an artist to use in printing lithographs.'

'Wash day was hard work in our early days. The copper was built into the corner of the scullery and had to be kept on the boil with wood and coal shovelled onto the fire beneath. In some houses in Leverstock Green the water had to be pumped up to fill the copper, which was also used to cook the Christmas puddings, which bounced about in the boiling water. Steam was everywhere. The old wooden-rollered hand mangle squeezed out the water and was used to flatten the sheets when dry and folded.

The kitchen range was the means of cooking and heating and was put to many uses. It had to be blackleaded each week – not a popular task with the young women of the family. The stove was usually draped with things to dry or warm, wet shoes steamed gently at the side, the kettle constantly hissed on the top, pots of stew bubbled away and the smell of baking in the oven wafted through the house.'

'In the 1920s a woman came in from Letchworth village at seven to light the huge copper fire with faggots. She washed all day, putting the clothes through a wooden mangle. She wore a cap and sacking apron and had beer and cheese for her dinner.'

'Not for me (and a lot more like me) going into a pastel tiled bathroom and turning on a tap. Things were somewhat different then. It all began early in the morning of bath night. Mother would get up very early and go downstairs to open the back door, June or January it made no difference, fresh air we were told was good for us and you didn't argue. Then she would put out in the yard, the strip of brown coconut matting from the scullery floor, the stool, which was in fact an old chair without its back, the lid from the top of the copper and the gingham curtain from round the brickwork of the copper. (This was considered by my friend to be posh, as her mother didn't have a curtain round hers.) After all this had taken place, Mother would fetch some newspaper and some sticks, and build a fire under the copper, which was a large brick construction built into the corner of the scullery. In the middle was a very large cauldron-type pot into which Mother would put cold water from the tap. She would then light the fire from some rolled up newspaper which she put under the kettle on the gas stove in the summer or lit from the range in the living room in winter. It was considered a waste to use a match if you had some naked flame already going.

When the fire was well under way, she would put into the water two handfuls of common soda, some grated household soap and some Rinso washing powder. Then in went the clothes, white cotton sheets first, and then in order of cleanliness, the rest of the week's washing. After washing came the rinsing, done in the sink or in a tin bath outside. The clothes would be put through the mangle, some would be put into Robin starch and the rest straight onto the washing line. Mother would use the water from the copper to scrub the scullery floor, the back yard and the front steps. Precious hot water was never wasted.

After the copper had been emptied, it was refilled with clean water. If there was soft rain water from the butt, this was preferred, but if not it was water from the tap. The fire under the copper was made up again and the second lot of water heated. This was the bath water. When I was very small, Mother would lift me straight into the copper before the water got too hot, wash me with the same Fairy washing soap, then sit me on the side of the brickwork to dry me. When I got bigger she would ladle the water into a tin bath which had been put before the fire in the living room. The towels were lovely and warm as they were put on the fireguard. While I was in the bath she would let me have the wireless on and listen to "Dick Barton Special Agent" and "In Town Tonight". She would also give me a spoonful of cod liver oil – it was to do me good, that's what I was told. If the water began to get cold she would

75

top it up with some more hot water. After I had been put to bed she would use my bath water with more hot in, then came Dad's turn. He had the job to ladle out some of the water until he could drag it to the back door, then put the rest down the outside drain, which Mum would then scrub with a huge scrubbing brush. The bath was then hung up on a nail in the shed until next time. Do you wonder this performance only took place once a week?'

'My memories of home life are vivid, from quite an early age. There was gaslight in our house but some of my friends' houses were lit by oil lamps. I have never forgotten the ritual of preparation of the oil, care of the fragile mantle, lighting of the wick under a tall glass shade, and oh! the smell.

There was no bathroom in our house when I was a small child. Bath night was every Saturday. A tin tub was placed in front of the living room fire and was filled with hot water from several large saucepans etc. Towels were warmed from the heat of the coal fire. Following a bath and hair wash, there was a weekly dose of opening medicine such as syrup of figs to be swallowed. A mixture of brimstone and treacle had to be taken in the spring to clear the blood, together with Dr Williams Pink Pills if you appeared to be on the pale side.'

'Most of us at Bayford lived in small two-bedroomed cottages with no electricity or water. Our earliest memories are of helping to fill the copper for washday and bathnight with buckets of water from a tap in the middle of the village. Imagine an average family of five children. The bath was placed in the living room in front of the fire and the cleanest went in first, the dirtiest last. Think of the arguments! We always had to be in bed early. We rose early too and some of us had to walk up to eight miles to school and back.'

THE SLIPPER BATHS

'We lived in a terrace house at Watford in the 1930s, with no bathroom and the toilet at the end of the garden. It was quite a performance putting on coat and shoes in the winter to go to the loo. I had to take a torch with me, but wouldn't shine it around much because of the huge spiders that seemed to lurk in there.

Sunday mornings I used to walk to the public slipper baths with my father, our clean clothes and towel and soap in a carrier bag.

If it was a busy morning there were many people waiting in a small room before the attendant called you to an empty cubicle. Each one had a huge white bath in it and a scrubbed stool and rubber mat. The water was turned on from outside by the attendant and the door had to stay open until she thought the water was deep enough; later during the war, five inches was all that was allowed and a mark was painted on the side of the bath. If the water was too hot or cold, there was a small bell you could push and shout out your requirements. There was no top to the cubicle. If you stayed in too long, the attendant knocked on the door asking you to hurry up, more people were waiting. Feeling all pink and damp I would then go to the small tea bar where my father was ordering cups of cocoa. I had strict instructions from my mother not to come out into the air until my pores had closed! Then a brisk walk home – my father did not believe in waiting around for buses.

Shortages and cuts later stopped the women's section being open on a Sunday, so I had to go on Wednesday afternoons instead. If not a washdown in the scullery had to do, when the foot bath was filled with water from kettles on the range. No locks on the doors, so it meant singing or whistling and splashing around to let the rest of the family know you were washing. The gas stove was lit in the winter and the oven door left open to make stripping off more comfortable, then one washed up as far as you could and down as far as you could with decency.'

FROM THE CRADLE
TO THE GRAVE

In the past you were much more likely to bear your children, suffer illnesses, and die in your own home. Many villages in the past had local women who were always called on to act as unofficial midwives or layers-out of the dead, until the District Nurse came gradually to take over from them and to bring modern medicine into the home. Home cures were always popular, though how efficacious they were is open to question! Some illnesses were more serious though, and diseases such as scarlet fever and polio claimed many victims in those 'good old days'.

BIRTH, MARRIAGE AND DEATH

'I can remember lying awake at night and hearing pebbles being thrown at the window which meant that someone had passed away, and my mother was needed to do what they called "laying-out". This was in the early 1900s at Bovingdon. As far as births were concerned, neighbours helped each other out over that without help from a doctor.'

A village wedding at Pirton c1920. The whole village celebrated with the happy couple. (Photograph courtesy of Hitchin Museum)

'Until I was eleven in 1918 I was an only child. Our neighbours had a very large family and there seemed to be a new baby every year. I used to go to the nurse and say, "You keep taking the babies there. They can't look after the ones they've got now – why don't you bring one to us?" She said, "Well, what do you want?" I said, "I'd like a sister but I don't mind". My mother must have been pregnant at this time, but I didn't know, and when the baby came I was so pleased I ran all round Ridge Hill telling everyone. I used to push him around in the pram; I took him to school to show the teachers and was most disappointed when they didn't get as excited as me. I expect they thought I was mad! I still thought the nurse had brought my brother and it was left to one of my school friends to tell me otherwise.'

'Straw would be put down in the streets to deaden the noise of horses' hooves and iron shod wheels when someone was very ill or dying.'

'Births took place mostly in the home in the 1930s and 1940s at Bayford, with the help of neighbours, friends and the village nurse. She was paid for by annual subscription and the proceeds of a summer fete. People were very close in those days, entire extended families lived within our village and were always on hand to share the joys and sorrows of all occasions.

Deaths also occurred mostly in the home. Most bodies were taken off on the final journey on a farm cart but the gentry had carriages with black horses with special plumes. There were many fatal farming accidents.

There was a lot of inter-marrying in our village and people were grateful for the war in at least bringing fresh blood into the village with evacuees and land girls.'

HOME CURES

'Home cures I remember include butter and sugar mixed together for colds on the chest, also camphorated oil rubbed on the chest. Vinegar and a blue bag were used for stings, and an onion was rubbed on chilblains.'

'Earache was treated with warm oil and camphorated oil. Syrup of figs seemed to cure everything!'

SCARLET FEVER AND POLIO

'At the age of six in the 1920s I had what was thought to be a bad bout of influenza, after which I was unable to stand. A "Specialist" was called in, who laid me on the table and manipulated my legs, stood me on the floor and told me to walk, whereupon I promptly fell into the fireplace. "Infantile Paralysis" was duly pronounced (polio) with the prognosis that I would probably never walk again. No further treatment was prescribed, but due to my mother's massage, wrapping my leg in Thermogen wool, and sheer determination I walked, albeit with a slight limp. My Grannie's Primrose Ointment was also used liberally and for any cuts or grazes. This she made by boiling up "hus licks" (house leeks) which she grew in an old frying pan on the shed roof, with lard from the local farm, and then added a basketful of primrose heads which we gathered from nearby woods. The resulting ointment was spooned into little jars, a layer of lard put on top and then a covering of brown paper tied with string and kept in a dark cupboard until spring came round again.

I resumed school at Chipperfield, at first for half days, transported by donkey's back, and then for full days, cycling the mile trip on a small bicycle made to measure by a clever man at Bovingdon.'

'In 1942 I had scarlet fever and had to go to the isolation hospital in Tolpits Lane (Holywell) for three months. Only my mother was at home, it being the middle of the war, and I was only two and a half and completely bewildered and distressed. I had no idea why I was there. I have memories of getting up in the middle of the night with no-one there and finding my way down cold concrete-floored corridors. My teddy bear was put in an incinerator.'

THE DISTRICT NURSE

'The health of Little Munden village was taken care of by our District Nurse and Midwife, the first arriving in 1907. Each in turn cycled round the area with her little black bag, covering many miles. Babies were born at home and mums were taken care of for a fortnight by Nurse. Many times Nurse was known to put a rice pudding in the oven together with potatoes to bake before she went on her rounds. A neighbour was engaged to do the washing and ironing – the washing alone was a day's work.'

'A committee of local ladies "ran" the District Nurse at Park Street and as my mother lived nearest to Nurse Mason, she would appear at the garden gate with any queries, keeping a wary eye on our terrior Kim, who hated officials in uniform.'

'Ethel May Grimwood was born in 1894. The eldest child in a family of 15, she was brought up by her grandparents and only came into contact with her brothers and sisters at school. At 14 she went into domestic service in Harpenden. This was regarded as a fortunate development only brought about by having an aunt who already worked at the house having spoken up for her. When she was 24 she decided to train as a nurse at Watford General Hospital. After three years general nursing training she went on for a further year to study midwifery. This was done as it could lead to her securing the position of a District Nurse and eventually a house with the job. In due course she acquired a post in the parish of Hertford Heath and Great Amwell. This was a widely spread area and her only means of transport was a bicycle. In the 1920s the District Nurse was required to attend to all age groups within the community from birth to terminal care.

Nurse Grimwood can be recalled reminiscing on an incident when a "man of the road" knocked on her door late one evening when it was pouring with rain. The tramp said 'Can you come missus?' She followed him to a piece of common land near Haileybury College known as The Roundings. There, under a blackberry bush, laying on a piece of old tarpaulin, was a woman in labour. Nurse decided she could not cope with the situation and needed assistance. After assuring him that there was time, she proceeded to a nearby public house where she got the landlord to telephone for an ambulance. The man was most annoyed when the ambulance arrived, but was finally persuaded that hospitalisation was essential. The woman was taken away and was safely delivered. Three days later, she was back in the village with her man, the new baby and their chattels in the pram and on the road again.

Nurse Grimwood's daughter recalls being told that there had been some difficulty with mothers from the village after Nurse had visited the school and sent some children home who had 'dirty' heads. On one occasion, horror of horrors, she had to send her own son home for the same reason. For the most part, however, the District Nurse was a loved member of the community.

Nurse Grimwood later met Jack Camp, a Haileybury college servant, who throughout her life she referred to as "the best man in the village". They eventually decided to marry and that the wedding would take place at her home in Suffolk. This presented something of a problem to the groom and his family in how to get to the wedding. It was decided to hire a 22 seater coach from Dye's of Hertford. For conveyance to the church they had a carriage and pair and the bride's bouquet was a bunch of sweet peas picked from a neighbour's garden. The reception was held in the village reading room at Tuddenham St Mary opposite the village green. It can be recalled that at one stage of the proceedings the two youngest boys, one from each of the families, had to be stopped from fighting around the village pump. Later one of the combatants was seen to be sporting "a shiner" as a result.

The inevitable then happened. Nurse Camp became pregnant. This necessitated her giving up "the District" and caused her to be fined by the local authority for failing to complete the number of years she had agreed upon.

The job that her husband was doing at Haileybury College was poorly paid – about £7 a month. At the time Nurse Camp could get about £12 a month when working. She obviously wanted to get back to nursing as quickly as possible. Eventually she succeeded in getting a District nursing post in the village of Gilston. She employed a 14 year old girl from Hertford Heath to go with the family to Gilston as a mother's help/nanny, thus enabling her to go about her nursing duties. She would say that she never knew what next would be coming to her door. Anything from a splinter under a fingernail to a wound from a shooting accident. However, midwifery gave her the most satisfaction. In those days babies were mostly born at home where few facilities existed. Expectant fathers were detailed off to make lots of hot water available. This was done by lighting a fire under the brick built copper in the scullery or shed or alternatively in a large pan on the kitchen range.

Nurse Camp was proud of the fact that throughout her career she managed to avoid having any cases of sepsis – quite an achievement in the circumstances.

By the time her children were seven and five, a Haileybury College servant's house became available at Woolens Brook. Previously her husband had been cycling each way daily between Gilston and the College. The opportunity to ease this journey was too much to resist. They moved into 1 Foster Cottages and she gave up the Gilston position. Nursing was still in her blood however, and after a time she got herself engaged on relief nursing work in the surrounding area. For a time she acted temporarily as the matron of Lansdowne House, a private nursing home in Broxbourne. Her first delivery at the home was twin girls. They were so small that they were wrapped in cotton wool and placed head to tail in a shoe box instead of a cot. The babies survived and the mother never forgot Nurse

Camp and always stopped to speak of their progress whenever they met. This was not an isolated happening. Men and women from all walks of life would call out to her when shopping and she would say proudly – "Oh, he's just one of my babies."

Even after her retirement people would come to ask her to lay someone out or stay with a prospective mother while waiting the arrival of the nurse or doctor. In fact on one occasion she did deliver a baby after she had retired because the regular nurse had been delayed on another difficult case. This was unusual and had to be recorded but no fuss ensued. Even in retirement she did not leave the nursing scene. For a few years she held down a part time job on an ambulance service which took patients with tuberculosis from Ware Park Sanatorium to various homes or hospitals. Incidentally she continued to ride her bicycle until well into her seventies. Once a nurse – always a nurse. Nurse Camp died of old age in 1978 aged 84.'

'I had finished my Midwifery training in the 1940s which had been done under contract, which meant I had to work for two years to part repay for my training.

I was sent off to a cottage hospital for one month, where I was to do any home nursing that was needed. I had to hire a car and a driver from the local garage and I was to be taught to drive while on my rounds. This was all happening in 1946 – there were very few cars on the road and petrol was rationed, so you can imagine what a wonderful time I had travelling round this beautiful countryside, not so lucky for the driver as he must have had some nervous moments. There were no driving instructors or schools in those days.

At the end of the month I was considered to be proficient enough to drive a car of my own. I reported back to the County Office to await my next assignment. To my great surprise, I was given the keys of a brand new Austin 8 and dispatched off to the large rural area of Belford which is on the Great North Road overlooking Holy Island. I was to live in the Nurses Home, which had been given originally by Countess Grey of Follodon. My head was now in the clouds, being one of the first nurses to be given a car to do my rounds, but there was a sting in all this.

The Health Service was being implemented and there were great changes taking place, no longer were communities supporting their local nurses and medical services, they were being financed by the new Health Service. My little car and I were part of this change and I was to take over my new area, where previously twelve nurses had been employed.

Because of the rural nature of the area the nurses had "lived in" and nursed the patients as long as was necessary. Now I was to visit them daily and had to instruct them as to the care that would be needed till my return visit. There was a great deal of apprehension at first, but we won through. Today we take this as normal as the public are much more informed, but this was a beginning.

All went well until the winter when we experienced the great snow storm of 1947. I awoke to find the Great North Road blocked by snow drifts the height of telephone poles.

I was snow bound – I managed to get a set of chains for the car and each day had to wait for the snow plough to open up a track and I followed behind. I had to leave the car at the roadside and walk to the house, sometimes waist deep in snow. The local people rallied round and dug out tracks to make it a little easier.

It was an exciting time, the countryside was a wonderful sight, the sun shone brilliantly each day and I was on duty during the whole period. I ran the car till the snow thawed and the chains fell off.

When I eventually got off duty I went to the theatre in Newcastle, but ended up at the Eye Hospital, I couldn't see anything. I had snow blindness!'

SHOPPING AND CALLERS TO THE DOOR

Food was plain and often home-grown, but the allure of home-cured bacon, fresh butter and free range eggs for the finding is still strong. From the muffin man to the butcher's boy, callers to the door could provide most of our everyday needs. Tradesmen knew that they needed to provide a good and reliable service to satisfy their customers, known to them personally, and even small villages saw a surprising number of commercial vehicles. Unless you lived in a town, market day was perhaps the only time when 'proper' shopping was considered.

PIGS AND BLOATERS

'As a young child in the 1920s holidays were spent on my uncle's mixed farm. Heavy horses were used for ploughing and all cultivation, harvesting etc. Milk was separated, the cream retained and the skimmed milk fed to the pigs – not the humans! The first milking after a cow calved was made into a baked custard. Delicious butter was also made in the dairy and the poultry were "free range". We picked primroses in nearby woods for Mothering Sunday and cowslips for making wine.'

'Our house at Lemsford in the 1940s had a large piece of ground at the side of it where we kept some chickens. My father decided to breed pigs as there was plenty of room, and when they were slaughtered I was taught how to remove the hair from the skin with boiling water and to rub in saltpetre to cure the meat. We also made lard and brawn. In fact we used every part of the pig. I used to love preparing their food which consisted of boiling small potatoes in an old copper and mashing them with bran. We also kept rabbits.'

'We had open fires and oil lamps. Bloaters from Watford market were a treat, cooked on a poker over the fire, with a fire-shovel arranged to catch the drips! The rector's sister came round once a fortnight to our house at Sarratt Bottom with a solid cold rice pudding as a gift – a way of using up spare milk from their cows.'

'The muffin man would come out to Park Street from St Albans on the train on a Friday afternoon, and he would go through the village with the muffin tray on his head supported by a sort of flat cushion, ringing his bell whilst we raced across the path to our house to herald the glad tidings to our family.

My father loved having people to lunch on the spur of the moment, and a frantic phone call would go to the butcher about twelve noon and up would come the butcher's boy with chops or whatever a few minutes later. We also went down to the watercress beds and loved walking along the thin boards for the big bunches.'

'I have fond memories of sitting on the common at the top of the hill at Wigginton waiting for the ice-cream man to struggle up the hill with his "Stop me and buy one" tricycle. Not for us a cone of soft ice cream from a van playing a jingle-jangle tune. We had a fruit flavoured water ice which we pushed up from the bottom through a triangular-shaped tube.

A popular packed lunch for the working man in the area was main course and pudding all in one. Called a Tring Clanger, this was a suet dumpling filled at one end with meat or bacon and with jam at the other. It was like two dumplings joined into one.'

'Mum was an excellent cook, in the home-cooking sense – steak and kidney puddings and pies, casseroles, roast dinners, plum duff, sponge puddings, apple pies, jams, marmalades, cakes, and Dad grew every kind of vegetable and soft fruits as well as apples, plums and pears. I have no recollection of anything coming out of a tin (except custard powder). We kept chickens and ducks (the river Beane runs at the bottom of the garden) and the eggs were pickled in isinglass.

Our milk was delivered daily by horse and cart carrying a huge churn from which we filled our milk jugs. No delivery on Sundays, so we children walked to the local farm and collected milk from the cows! Occasionally in the summer the Walls ice cream man would come along on his bike with a large box on the front and we would run out to the road with excitement for this treat.'

'Stockmen at Redbourn tended cattle, sheep and pigs. A good stockman would be given a side of fat pork which was salted and hung in an outhouse. Rashers were sliced off as required. The chitterlings were put into a bucket of salt water placed by the fire and turned over every day until thoroughly clean. Pork fat was diced, heated and the lard drained off, then pressed to make crinklings for eating. Sometimes they were made into crinkling cakes.

Milk, straight from the cow, was put into pans and the cream skimmed off to make butter. Children had to help by shaking the churn whenever they had a spare minute.

Most homes had a vegetable plot, otherwise there were allotments at Dudley and Brache so there was always a good supply of fresh produce. Many families kept chickens and those living near the Common had ducks and geese which were allowed to graze on the Common with goats and horses. Surplus produce was given away or sold. Gooseberries were measured in a pint jug and cherries by the pottle. A pottle was a round wooden straight-sided bowl holding half a gallon. Apples and potatoes were measured in bushel baskets and smaller quantities sold by the peck.

The milkman made daily deliveries in his pony and cart which carried two large milk churns. The milk was measured in half or one pint ladles and poured into the customer's own jug as she stood on her doorstep. The baker also delivered daily carrying an assortment of loaves in a large bread basket. Hot cross buns were seven for sixpence. One baker's roundsman had a bicycle with a huge container over the front wheel like the ice-cream man. Our favourite ice-cream seller was Jimmy Bolino, a one-armed gentleman affectionately known as "Okey Pokey" and always to be seen on the common when cricket was being played.

The lamplighter made his round by bicycle, balancing a long pole as he rode – one tug with his pole and the light appeared. Gas was supplied to some houses but often only downstairs, so candles were used at bedtime. Fragile gas mantles were always handled with great care.'

BROUGHT TO THE DOOR

'Food was always plentiful and good. We kept hens at Belsize and grew all our own vegetables. At first I used to fetch milk in a can from the local farm, together with their own cream, cheese and butter, but then a delivery man called. Home-made wine, usually cowslip or dandelion, was usually bubbling in the corner.

Later in my childhood in the 1920s local traders came; the butcher from Flaunden – called the "midnight butcher" as he usually came after calling at the pub, and the oil-man from Bovingdon, who also later changed the accumulators for the wireless. The baker came every morning – Hot Cross Buns, seven for sixpence, were delivered warm before breakfast on Good Friday. Ethel Spool's home-made custard icecream from Chipperfield was legendary. After Sunday school I would call for a basinful for threepence and then pedal home like mad on my bike before it melted.

Most of our shopping was done in Sarratt, especially at the Miss Friends', who kept the post office and were very strict. I remember once Granny had not put her cross on her pension book, and we were made to walk the mile back to Belsize for the mark, and back again to collect the money.'

'Transport to town from Little Munden in the 1910s was a carrier's cart which went to town each Saturday and seats were limited so booking in advance was essential. The carrier also called for the papers and we had to meet him for ours on his return to the village; the children's newspapers, a comic, a daily paper, the weekly district news in *The Mercury*, and *The Ringing World*, the latter being a paper for bellringers which was passed round among the ringers each week.

Shopping was largely done through door to door salesmen who came at regular intervals. The draper came with his case displaying one each of many varieties of clothing, from liberty bodices, combinations and knickers to blouses, stockings and socks, lace-up boots (no wellingtons then) and slippers. Orders were taken and the goods sent on approval the following week. The grocer called fortnightly, always leaving a few sweets "for the kids", and the butcher came weekly, taking the order for the next week at the same time. Milk from the farm, in a can, and skimmed milk could be purchased at twopence a quart.'

'My uncle, Mr Alec Clarke, had a milk round in Wormley in the 1930s. The highlight of my young life was when he let me ride on the milk float with him. There was a big brass churn at the front, which in the summer had a white cover on it. We used to fill a milk carrier from this and go to the customer's door. We would dip a measure into the carrier, and pour the milk into the jug which the customer had brought to the door. The jug was often covered with a net circle edged with beads, to keep out the flies. No fridges in those days! We used to make these covers from old net curtains and a broken string of beads.'

'I can still see Mrs Richardson, the milkman's wife, going around Welwyn village on her three-wheeled tricycle. This had a compartment on the side in which stood a small churn of milk and a measuring can which had a straight spout, used to pour our milk into a jug. After this I think bottles must have started, with cardboard tops. One day her daughter was on the round and Blow's (the builders) sand lorry came up our narrow lane and dragged her off the tricycle. She was brought into our house until the doctor came, her arm ripped from shoulder to elbow. It left her with a terrific scar.

Another thing we had in my early days was the coal and clothing club. This was run by Mrs Giles and her sister who lived at the Manor House. They would sit in the village hall on Mondays from twelve noon to one o'clock. It was always my job to go and pay this for my mother when I came home from school. Most people managed to pay sixpence, but there might have been the odd shilling paid if mums were able to afford it. This was paid out in the autumn so at least there was money for a bag or two of coal and a pair of shoes for the children in which to start the winter.'

'The milkman at Northchurch in the late 1930s (Sonny Vincent by name) had a cart pulled by a horse called "Philip". When he arrived in our road we would all help Sonny deliver the milk (about six of us) scurrying hither and thither up our steep hill. At the top we all climbed on to the cart with churns and crates and with a flick of the reins Philip and the cartload would charge down the hill and up the other side just as steep. We often stayed on the cart for the rest of the round and rode back to the depot (Storey's Dairy) in Northchurch along the main A41. It subsequently turned out that the man I eventually married who had lived on the other side of Berkhamsted had helped the same milkman, with the same horse, but on the early part of his round. We never met because those children departed before Sonny reached our side.'

'In the 1920s and early 1930s at Cheshunt I can remember the milkman coming daily to our back door with a huge churn from which he ladled milk, be it the pint or half pint. The baker called daily and the butcher. A fishmonger cried out "Fresh herrings" and an oil man came once a week with soaps, candles, oil etc.'

'Travelling salesmen around Hemel Hempstead included the winkle man, horse-drawn milk and bakery carts, ice-cream bikes, the muffin man calling out "Muffins and crumpets", and hot cross buns sold in the street in Leverstock Green. A Mrs Plummer in Ebberns Road made and sold pease pudding. Home made ice cream cost a half-penny a cornet. Two ladies remember buying "skate's eyeballs" – the flesh at the wingtips – from Brinklow's on their way home from Girl Guides in the wartime black-out.'

The first Co-op shop in Hemel Hempstead c1906. The Co-op and its 'divi' soon became a part of family life.

'There were four working farms at Burnham Green in the 1930s and 1940s, and I remember fetching the milk from Burgess's Farm for twopence halfpenny. I also fetched the milk for a lady who gave me a halfpenny for going.

We had a small village shop but mostly we were served by local traders from Old Welwyn and Old Stevenage. There was "Phil the Baker" who came from Coulson's in Old Welwyn in his horse and trap to deliver the bread, and someone came round on Saturday mornings with sausages for Saturday lunch. Mr Thody from Welwyn, the fishmonger, used to visit the village twice a week and shout "Alive-o, alive-o". He would let my mum have a big bag of sprats for sixpence and "us kids" a bag of winkles for a penny. Mr Day from Old Stevenage was the butcher.'

VILLAGES AND SMALL COUNTRY TOWNS

'Berkhamsted is now a town with a population of about 15,000, but I remember it as a small country town, where everyone seemed to know everyone else, or at least know someone connected to them.

There were all kinds of tradesmen, some had shops which had belonged to their fathers and so, if you had lived in the town all your life, they probably knew your parents as well as they knew you.

What services they offered. Bakers coming to your door every day with real bread – how one loved the crusty loaves, with lots of butter and home-made jam. Along Ellesmere Road, where I lived, we had a muffin man come every Saturday afternoon from Hemel Hempstead, he with his lovely white apron on, a small pad on his head on which to carry his tray of muffins and crumpets. He had a wonderful loud bell to ring whilst holding onto his tray with his other hand, seven crumpets for sixpence, and what a treat they were on a cold winter's afternoon.

There was also the vegetable man with his horse and cart, loaded, or it seemed, with the very freshest vegetables and fruit it was possible to have. He was always ready to tell you which was the best buy for that day.

The milkman called twice a day, measuring his milk from a churn with his brass measure, and one could get a half a pint, or even a quarter pint of milk if one wished. The cream was kept in a large china bowl, this he measured with a gill measure. The fish-man called twice a week. They collected their fish from Berkhamsted railway station, hence there was a passage at the station which always smelt of fish, one never walked through it. The fish was put there to be collected, and the empty boxes were taken back.

Butcher boys would come on their bikes to the house for orders, and would even bring the ordered meat back in time to cook that day for lunch. Otherwise it was brought the next day.

Kinghams the grocer (now Waitrose) came for their order Tuesday and delivered Thursday, and Thursday's order was delivered Saturday. The book for the grocer was made up ready for when he called.

One of my earliest recollections was of the paraffin-man; he had a pony and trap and he came on a Friday evening. This particular evening it had been raining and some of the oil had been spilled on the ground, and by the light of the gaslamp nearby it reflected lovely colours on the road. This pattern of colour made a lasting impression. I remember too on Saturdays how one always tried to go to the High Street where the market stalls were (and still are) and the flower stalls full of colour. In the early days before the war, on Saturday evenings all the local village folk used to come to the town by bus, to shop at the stalls, the streets were packed with people and most of the trade was done then. In those days it was 9pm before they cleared away their stalls.

Young men and girls dressed in their best clothes used to parade up and down the High Street. There were no problems with so many youngsters about, they were all too busy trying to attract each other's attention.'

'As a child during the 1940s I recall how interesting it was to watch the tradesmen's horses pulling their brightly painted carts along the high street at Berkhamsted, after collecting their goods from the local shops and dairies. One of the bakers had three horses and vans which could be seen lined up at the kerbside at lunch time waiting for the next batch of hot bread for the afternoon delivery.

These horses knew their "rounds" and at which house they automatically stopped and were handed an apple or sugar lump! As this is a hilly town the coal merchants used two large shire horses to pull the coal carts up the hills. These horses were specially shod to prevent them from slipping. When they eventually reached the top of the hill and were on level ground, one horse was let out of the shafts of the cart and tethered to the back of the cart containing the empty sacks, to return to the coal-yard for re-loading. The feed bags and water buckets were hung on the carts and when the drivers had their break, the horses were given their feed bags to munch and toss – not to miss a single oat!

British Rail, or the LMS railway as it was then known, had large covered wagons as well as open carts, to make deliveries to the shops direct from the goods trains for distribution. These horses had very impressive harnesses with a lot of jangling horse brasses. Equally the large horses which pulled the barges along the tow-paths of the Grand Union Canal, which were laden with coke, coal and timber. It was a joy to see these huge horses waiting patiently by the locks while the water levels rose and fell, so they could proceed again on their way.

One can still see some of the old stables behind the

shops in the High Street, where the horses were stabled during their working week until Saturday, when they would be led to a quiet field for a well earned rest.'

'On a Tuesday it was not unusual to see animals being driven through the streets of Watford to the cattle market then held in Stones Alley, just off Market Street. As a child I can remember being taken to see the sheep, cows etc in the pens. Thank goodness I did not realise then that some would be taking the short walk to the abattoir. The shopkeepers disliked the animals being driven through the main streets as on occasions a scared beast would bolt into a shop. My husband can remember a bullock charging into Lawley's China Shop (the origin of a bull in a china shop perhaps?) and doing untold damage. I too remember seeing an animal disappear into a shop in Clarendon Road when I was with my mother and we watched events with interest from the safety of the Palace Theatre steps.

Shopping used to be a much more leisurely affair and the shops remained a fixture over many years. I used to love being taken into a draper's shop called Percy Wilson's in the High Street on the corner of Water Lane. A chair was provided for the customer to sit at the counter whilst an assistant produced a selection of the required items from a neat little drawer taken from a whole wall of drawers at the back of the counter. The highlight for me was when the assistant took the money and popped it, with a written bill, into a metal container above her head and pulled a lever sending the cylinder flying on a wire above our heads to a central cash desk and then back it would come seconds later with any change and a receipted bill. It was like an aerial railway with containers flying in all directions. Cawdell's Department Store had a similar system but the cylinders went through a pipe which wasn't nearly so exciting. Their cylinders dropped

On market day the country came to town. This view of Watford Market c1908 shows the sheep pens set out in the main street.

down into a container on the return trip with a loud noise which could make you jump with fright if you were not prepared for it.

Delivery was then part of the service given by shops. Imagine today going into a shop, purchasing a pair of corsets (or stays, as they were then called), and asking for them to be delivered! One member remembers her husband having a job in his youth as a delivery boy at a draper's called Beales in Queen's Road and having to deliver such items. She also remembers that the box containing stays, a long-shaped one, made a good container for knitting needles.'

'At the time of the Second World War there were three grocer's shops in Aldbury, one of which had a bakehouse where bread and cakes were baked to be delivered around the village. There was a post office where stationery and toys could be bought, and a general store where literally anything could be found, from pins and needles, through clothes, electrical goods and garden equipment. Milk was delivered by a local farmer straight from the dairy. There was also a policeman in the village, in a house that included a cell.'

'My mother bought most of her groceries from W B Moss & Sons who had a shop in Nightingale Road, Hitchin in the early 1950s. An assistant would call at our house for the order once a week and the goods would be delivered next day by an errand boy on a bicycle with a carrier at the front. We had bread delivered every day by a local baker, but most of our fruit and vegetables were home grown.'

'Tradesmen called regularly at our house. The postman made three daily deliveries with the exception of Sundays. The milkman called twice a day. He drove a milk cart carrying shiny churns. Whilst he filled a jug with creamy frothing milk, his horse waited patiently for a sugar lump. On occasions the milkman would pat up yellow butter into half pound packs. The baker brought a basket to the door filled with a large assortment of crusty loaves, six days a week. The butcher boy came on his bicycle for a daily order for meat, to say nothing of a grocery delivery twice weekly, together with greengrocery and fish. What a wonderful service to the people of a small town. All of this was supplemented by a Wednesday market – Canary bananas sold by the "hand" about 20 for sixpence.

'I suppose the centre of Little Gaddesden village, being nearer the school and village hall, was the post office, at that time in the early 1950s a newsagent's as well as post office. Along the Green was Miss Pratt's, very popular with the children on their way to and from school; Miss

Pratt with her assistant, Louise, served groceries, and sweets.

At the Manor House was a market gardener and it was possible to buy vegetables there. Tucked away in a tiny cottage by Little Gaddesden House were Mr and Mrs Quennell. Mr Quennell sold everything from sweets to hardware; I still have 40 years on, an enamel chamber pot I bought. After some years they moved away and Mrs Peachy in another cottage took over the sweet business. This was another popular venue for the school children for many years. Mrs Peachy used to welcome the kiddies, who enjoyed showing her the drawings and paintings they had done at school. She used to serve sweets in little

The village shop, such as The Top Shop at Standon in the 1920s, was often the backbone of village life.

screw packs, there were also a lot of cats there.

At this time there were two butchers who delivered their goods, one of them had a shop at Hudnall. Two bakers, one from Dagnall and one from Potten End, who delivered on alternate days, and two milkmen, Express and Mr Underwood. Sainsbury's and Kinghams grocers also collected and delivered orders. The Co-op van was a regular for many years and catered for practically all our needs.

Then Mr McIntyre began to come round with his Trojan van; he supplied groceries and sweets. I used to buy marmalade and jam from him in large seven pound crock jars. Unfortunately as he came on Wednesdays, it was sometimes difficult to find pennies for the children's sweets, but he was a kind man. There was another man who walked from goodness knows where, carrying a basket filled with haberdashery, and I used to feel compelled to purchase some small item. My workbox still holds a collection. The gipsies also came regularly; they had slices of bread and jam on the back doorstep and were rather a nuisance until we had a bulldog, the gentlest of animals but he looked ferocious. Alas with so called progress in the early 1960s the shops began to disappear. With people affording cars to go to Hemel and Berkhamsted to do their shopping, it was no longer viable for deliveries to be made. We have one shop left, a mini supermarket and post office and the milkman comes three times a week.'

SHOPPING IN ST ALBANS

'We lived in Bernard Street, St Albans during the 1940s. Across the road and down a little way was a small greengrocer's where I was sent to purchase vegetables if none were available from the allotment. The allotment was behind the old prison, which is now the station car park.

My father worked on the railway, his office was beside the old engine shed and sidings. What a joy to go on to the footplate of a real steam train! Or into the South Box to be shown how the signal worked and watch the trains go by. I suppose we should not have been there really, but it was always a special treat.

I was sent shopping to the local grocer's – Lupton's – on the corner of Etna Road and Catherine Street to purchase loose biscuits. What delights our eyes beheld, sugar weighed by the pound, loose, and put into cones of blue paper or bags. Butter patted into shape with wooden boards, and grocery coupons! Mum having fruit etc when available, put by to make a Christmas cake or birthday cake for my brother or myself. Shelves and shelves of tinned goodies which made the eyes boggle, all neatly stacked and priced. The sweet shop on the opposite corner where we were allowed to spend our sweet coupons. Next door were Stawfords the butcher's, then Clarks the baker's. The Wool Shop that sold everything, from hooks and eyes, buttons and bows, to wool stacked on the shelves from floor to ceiling in arrays of colour, amazing to look at.

Further up Catherine Street was Warwicks with its displays of wet fish, and pheasants, rabbits and hares hanging from hooks in the ceiling when in season.

Then round the corner into St Peters Street, firstly the ABC bakers, where we were sent to queue for chocolate marshmallow sponge on a Saturday morning!

St Peters Street itself was a treat with its Tudor build-ings and Georgian-type facades. One such Tudor building housed Butlers, the butcher's, which was pulled down years later to extend Tesco's supermarket. Pamphilons, the drapers and furniture store on the corner of Adelaide Street where my mother and I queued to purchase a new bed for my brother, his very first, with saved up utility coupons, was a wonderful shop with its Tudor-style outside and dark stained wood fittings inside, so fresh and clean. Then further down the street, beside British Home Stores, was the lane up to the Cattle Market where we were taken to see the animals before they were sold.

Down St Peters Street and through into Market Place, at the start of French Row, a beautiful Tudor building housed Buglers the baker's. You went through the shop and up a central dark oak staircase to the coffee shop, in my teens a meeting place on Saturday mornings with friends for coffee and toasted tea cakes. Next door in French Row itself was the pork shop where I used to buy the pork pies and chitterlings for my father.

Then there was Fisks (where Heritage Close is now), an Aladdin's cave of materials, buttons, furniture, clothing – a good general department store, but to us children somewhere to browse and look around. Favourite was to sit on high stools to look through the books to choose patterns for perhaps a party dress or coat, and then to select the material to make it. A dark wooden fitted store, I remember, but oh so friendly. Window displays of dresses and coats dazzled a youngster's eyes, like fairyland.

If you couldn't obtain what was wanted at Fisks, then it was round the corner into Chequer Street to W S Green, a shop I remember where one had to keep going upstairs and downstairs to reach various departments.

One shop I have left until last, back in St Peters Street and that was Sainsbury's, a vast cathedral-like shop, in my eyes like a huge baronial hall, with counters down either side of its length, with high glass fronts. Tiled walls, with marble shelves, with big rounds of cheese waiting to be cut, and large pats of butter, so clean, and helpful assistants. At the very end of the shop a large panelled area, which I think was probably the desk and offices, but I never got down that far.'

CHILDHOOD &
SCHOOLDAYS

A COUNTRY CHILDHOOD

It is easy to forget how deep in the country were many of Hertfordshire's villages in the first decades of this century. Unspoiled lanes, fields and woods were the playground for generations of children, who wandered away for the day without fear and untroubled by motorised traffic. No wonder the sun always shines in our memories of those lost days.

LONG SUMMER DAYS

'My mother's memories went back to the end of the 19th century. As a small child she was taken by her mother to glean corn from the harvest fields, this to be fed to the hens. Most country people kept poultry in their back gardens to provide them with fresh eggs and so augment their small income. The highlight of her early life was the annual Sunday school outing which usually entailed a journey by horse and cart to woodlands and a festive high tea. With the advent of charabancs they ventured further afield, even to the coast to paddle in the sea with long dresses hitched up.'

'Hertfordshire to me is a small village named Aston, about three miles from Knebworth. A small boy called Stanley and I were sent to stay with his Granny Milton during the summer holidays. The year was 1918.

The house was very old. It had roses around the front door, which was never used, and an archway in the garden of everlasting sweet peas. There were apple trees and a lovely hedge of gooseberry bushes. We fetched the milk in a large can from a local farmer and walked down Aston End to see Farmer Clarke.

All the water for domestic use came from a neighbour's well down the lane. There was one at the front of the cottage but it had obviously dried up. We loved collecting the eggs from wherever the chickens decided to lay them.

We once walked to Old Stevenage and back to go to a fair; a long way for young legs. I well remember the dare we had from the village children to run around one of the churchyard tombs seven times when the Devil would appear on top. Needless to say, we ran off well before the terrible event happened. We watched the cricketers on the village green and paddled in Stony Ford. I still have a scar on one of my fingers where I cut myself on a broken bottle thrown in the water.'

'Comparing the day-to-day happenings in today's world with those I remember in my early years, makes me realise how lucky I was to grow up when I did. I think the earliest thing that stands out in my mind was going to the nearby park to feed the ducks, before I started school at five. I could walk just round the corner with my dog and doll. Mother had no need to worry about my being molested or harmed in any way. After a while, I would perhaps feel thirsty or want to see my mum and go home again with the dog. My mother would say "Where's dolly?" I would reply "Oh, she's all right." I had left her sitting on a seat in the park, because I was going back soon. Everything was all right, sitting just where I had left her.

From the age of seven, my father would give me a shilling when he came home in the evening, to go to the corner shop to buy an ounce of tobacco, a box of matches and an evening paper; there would be a ha'penny over which I could spend on sweets. It was quite "posh" to buy a ha'porth – they were put in a bag; it was possible to buy a farthing's worth but they were put in a conical bag made out of newspaper.

It was around this time, before the First World War, that I remember driving through Hyde Park in a horse-drawn carriage; my grandmother's brother was "well to do" and able to give such treats.

At this period before 1914, I remember coming out to St Margarets, to stay with friends of my father. We would have a picnic lunch, sitting at the edge of the cornfield which was being cut by horse-drawn plough. As the plough reached the centre all the rabbits would run out and I was sad to see them shot. My father used to row us on the river Lea, between St Margarets and Rye House; there were lots of long weeds in the water which were thought to be very dangerous, particularly for swimmers. Further down the river, horses pulled barges laden with timber, which was stacked along the banks getting thoroughly "dried out" before being used for furniture and house-building.'

'An 80 year old Abbots Langley man talked to us of his childhood and school holidays when he and several pals would take a packed lunch and walk miles, sometimes to Boxmoor Common, sometimes to Chipperfield or Kings Langley. They would pick wild raspberries or blackberries, or just explore and climb. They bird-nested, but only ever allowed one egg per nest to be taken. They would also go sparrow catching for halfpence from a local farmer. If they could, they scrumped apples and pears, but there were large dogs where the pear trees were.

As a growing youth he went to The Boys Home public house where all the young lads were initiated into this man's world of pubs. He graduated to The Green Man at Bedmond, where a muscular roadman had his own corner armchair and woe betide anyone who sat in it!

On Sundays he had to go to morning and evening

service and to Sunday school as well. Far more popular with the youngsters were the Treat teas which the local big house owners would vie with each other to put on, and smaller children had the vicarage garden teas.'

'When I was a five year old girl in the 1920s I used to visit my grandparents Mr and Mrs Bright at Waltham Cross where they had a hardware shop and forge. My grandfather being a blacksmith, I was allowed on special occasions to help him blow the bellows to make bright embers. I had a particularly pretty white dress and when I entered the forge my lovely grandfather would sing –

> Here comes the little girl
> Dressed all in white
> Blacksmith, Blacksmith
> Make the fire bright.

I also stayed with my grandparents overnight when my parents went out in the evening and clearly remember my grandfather in his nightshirt, kneeling by his bed saying his prayers night and morning.'

'I spent the early years of my life in a tiny cottage on the farm at Harpenden and still remember one of the great joys of my life was when Gran had a weak lamb wrapped up in front of the kitchen range and I was allowed to help with the bottle feeding. Another memory of those days comes to mind, how when a member of the family or close neighbour died, we had to go and tap the hive and tell the bees, or there would be no honey that year.

The highlight of summer at this time, early 1920s I suppose, was when Grandad hired a brake as it was called, and with the whole family in our Sunday best, we climbed aboard complete with picnic and spent a wonderful day at Bricket Wood. After my father returned from the First World War we moved and he worked on a much larger estate and life settled into a fairly normal routine. I went off to the village school in long black lace up boots and starched pinafore, as did so many other small girls at that time.

At night we made our own pastimes with cards, dominoes, board games etc. We were never allowed to waste time. My dad who wrote beautiful copperplate writing would sit and teach us children how it was done. Mum, who was a trained dressmaker, stitched for what I believe was called Queen Mary's Needlework Guild, and was keen that I should sew too. This Guild was run by the lady of the estate and the shirts, pyjamas, bedsocks etc that we made were sent to the London hospitals. I used to button-hole stitch bedsocks and at one time at the age of nine was one of the youngest people sewing for this cause.

Gathering dandelions for wine, blackberries for jam, gleaning corn and bagging it up for the chickens' winter feed and working in the garden has instilled in me the love of the land that I am every grateful for and although life was hard I had a very happy life as a child.'

'There were some things you never see now, such as the stallion being taken round the shire horses, his coat polished and shining, ribbons in his mane and tail, and the groom also polished and shining, bowler hatted as he led his huge charge from farm to farm. Up the lane about a mile and a half from our home at Park Street the hardy Yule breed of Arab horses were kept and would be brought down the lane on leading reins. We used to ride our Shetland pony up the lane and we were terrified of coming face to face, so to speak, with these beautiful creatures. It was up the hedge for us, whilst the beauty queens swept by.

I can remember bathing in the river Ver in November

with friends and having nothing to wear except a vest. It was cold but enjoyable.'

'A ford in the river at Sarratt was known as The Splash and when motorbike rallies came through, or the Hunt, I would open the big gate at the other end of the track for them and be rewarded with sixpence. Lovely summer days were spent paddling in the Chess and catching minnows. Having had quite a solitary childhood, I was frightened when I went to school in Sarratt, it was so noisy and there were so many children rushing about.'

'In the 1910s we used to fetch our milk in cans from Potterells dairy at Welham Green, where they had a herd of Jersey cows, and later on we fetched it from Potterells Farm where Mr Crawford lived. Among happy memories are the lovely haymaking days and all the picnics in the hay, and catching tiddlers in the stream nearby. We also went gleaning for the left over corn in the fields for our chickens which a lot of us kept in our back yards, in our case along with rabbits, a ferret and a jackdaw. We looked forward to the fetes at North Mymms Park, Potterells, Abdale and Hawkshead House, and to Brownies, Girls Guides, Scouts and Cubs. We used to do country dancing and dancing round the maypole.'

'Children at Redbourn often collected and chopped firewood and gathered mushrooms, blackberries and hazel nuts and went gleaning after the corn had been stooked to get feed for the chickens.

There were some poor children in the village who always had secondhand clothes and shoes given them at school, but we were well dressed, often in hand-made clothes. A luxury was to wear Mr Lawson's made to measure button-up boots. For winter warmth we wore

Many children remember dancing round the maypole on the village green. Here at Letchworth c1908 the local bobby keeps a benevolent eye on the proceedings. (Photograph courtesy of Hitchin Museum)

combinations, thick long legged knickers and liberty bodices. The draper always displayed a model wearing a liberty bodice. The first appearance of suspenders caused great interest and inquisitive children lifted skirts to get a peep.'

'The four younger girls in my family were great ones for going for long walks in the countryside around Bengeo where we lived. We would take a few jam sanwiches and a bottle of water and go off nearly all day. We were, I am ashamed to say, great collectors of wild flowers in the 1930s and we always won the wild flower competitions at school.

In 1946 my mother and I moved into a very large and draughty vicarage. It was an idyllic place for a child, surrounded by fields and with a large overgrown garden.

We had two prisoners of war (Italians) to tend the vegetable patch and they were with us until 1948 when they returned to their homeland.

My best friend, Margaret, lived next door in the vicarage cottages. I was envious of her because they didn't have a bathroom as we did, but bathed on Friday nights in a large tin bath in front of the blackleaded range. The bath was filled up with hot water which had been heated in zinc buckets on the range and "topped up" as each person finished bathing. How cosy, I thought, they don't have to put up with a cold and draughty bathroom. Their toilet was down the garden; an earth closet with two seats, one large, one small, with squares of newspaper to serve as loo roll. When I went to play with Margaret I always made the excuse to use their "lav" – to me at the age of eight it was far superior to our flush version!

On long summer days during the school holidays we went fishing for tiddlers and sticklebacks armed with a jam jar on which was tied a long piece of string. We lay for many hours in the long grass of the river bank waiting for a catch, and there were great cries of glee when we caught one. Saturday afternoons Margaret's father would take us ferreting. He kept two ferrets and we would go into the woods adjoining the vicarage, put nets over the rabbit holes, put a ferret down the hole, and with any luck a rabbit would run out of the opposite hole to be caught in the net, duly killed and taken home for rabbit stew. This was in the days before myxomatosis practically wiped out the rabbit population in many areas.

Autumn is a time of harvest, and many good things can be found in the hedgerows, including blackberries and crab apples. My mother used to make the most wonderful crab apple jelly. Early in the mornings, when the mist still hovered over the fields, we would go out and gather mushrooms with the dew still on them, and take them home for breakfast. These were the days before artificial fertilizers and sprays, when manure was manure and without which we wouldn't have our mushroom harvest.'

'At Westmill in the 1940s all the edges of the lanes were unkerbed, and the roads were covered with loose shingle on tar. The tar melted in the summer and stuck to the crepe soles and heels of my Clark's sandals – always brown and always with the "paw print" cut out on the upper.

I would sit beside my grandfather in his milk cart and hold the horse's reins as he measured out the milk from the churn to the waiting jugs.

Often I went walking along deserted country lanes early in the morning with our collie dog, and at seven years old I had no fears and no reason to worry. We paddled and even bathed in the river Rib, picking and eating the wild watercress without any thought of contamination or pollution – even though the water meadows were grazed by herds of cows! We went blackberrying, armed with old saucepans, paper bags and a long stick to pull the wayward branches down to eager fingers, branches drooping with the weight of those small, sweetest berries. The village fete, held in the Bury grounds, would display rows and rows of Kilner jars full of wild flowers picked from abundant hedgerows.

I had my first taste of banana after the Second World War from the first delivery to our village shop – what a disappointment!'

GAMES, TREATS AND SWEETS

With little motorised traffic about before the Second World War, children could play safely in the roads and lanes, spinning tops, bowling hoops and chalking out their hopscotch squares. Games followed time honoured rules and needed little equipment – essential when many parents could ill afford to buy their children new toys. They came in seasons too, as surely as the seasons of the year. Treats for yesterday's children would seem tame to their counterparts today, and a holiday was a rare luxury.

THE GAMES WE PLAYED

'In the early years of the century we girls wore a pinafore over our dresses, with black stockings and button boots. Men wore corduroy trousers tied under the knee with string and flannel collarless shirts to work.

Our games consisted of marbles, whip and top, hoops and hopscotch. There was no traffic and we played in the roads. We went wassailing at Christmas and singing on May Day. Our Sunday school outing was a trip on a farm waggon to Howes Retreat at Felden.'

'The year was marked by games in seasons. Dabbers was a favourite, where five stones were thrown up and caught on the back of the hand, with variations – "clap ones, clap twos" and "creepy crawlies"and lots of other variations enlivened the game and could of course be played anywhere. Marbles, tops with a stick and a piece of string, skipping and hopscotch on the road were other favourites, and rounders on the little green at Sarratt, using our coats as bases and a stick from the hedgerow as a bat.'

'We had chores to do but there was time for games. Favourites were hoops, tops, skipping and hopscotch. The hopscotch champion at Redbourn used a piece of slate – always closely guarded and never lent. Similarly the five pebbles for dabbers were very carefully chosen and secretly hidden when not in use. A ball thrown against a wall gave endless pleasure to those playing tens, a complicated routine of throwing and catching. Boys often made go-carts using old boxes fixed onto pram wheels.'

'On our way to the station at Welwyn North we had to pass Kit Nash's cottage at Harmer Green. We used to run past as fast as our legs would carry us. We were scared of her. She was the Hertfordshire Poacher who shot at a policeman, and she died in 1930 and is buried in Digswell churchyard. After her death we still used to run past the dilapidated cottage.

We amused ourselves playing hopscotch with a "tolly" (a piece of slate or tile) on the road, whipping our tops covered with silver paper from sweet wrappers. This made them pretty as they spun.'

'On Saturday mornings we all had some jobs to do, such as cleaning brasses etc, to earn our "Saturday penny" usually spent at Walsworth sweet shop. We might get four different things with a penny, such as sherbet fountains, love hearts with messages on, gobstoppers which changed colour as you sucked them, various liquorice assortments, and my favourite – a flat brittle boiled sweet about the size of the top of a tea cup, vinegar flavoured, we called them vinegar flats. We took them home and broke them into small pieces with the aid of a kitchen knife and the poker.

We played all sorts of games, including "jinks" played with five smooth stones to be tossed up and caught on the back of the hand, whip and top, hoops guided with a stick (some were wooden ones and some were steel), marbles mostly played in the gutter, skipping and hopscotch. Most of these games were played in the road as there was not a lot of traffic about in those days, and of course we went fishing in the river for tiddlers. Not always with a net, sometimes with a piece of cloth held by two children and swept under the riverweed to catch the tiddlers to be taken home in a jam jar with a home-made string handle.

My mother made a lot of our clothes when we were young and I remember well one outfit my sister and I had for school was a tweed skirt which was attached to a cotton bodice over which was worn a fair-isle jumper. However, the jumpers had a V neck, not really warm enough in winter, so mother cut out a piece of the tweed to be fastened in the V neck. I don't know about stopping us getting cold on the chest, it was certainly very itchy.'

'A ball game was played to "One, two, three o'lary, my ball's down the dairy, one, two three o'lary", bouncing the ball and at the end of the o'lary you threw your leg over the ball, trying to do it twice at the end. There were hoops, tops, skipping, conkers and, of course, "fag cards".'

'If there had been a library in Abbots Langley when I was growing up in the 1930s I doubt if I would have been allowed to use it. My mother was concerned about the risk of catching diseases from grubby library books, so using Watford library was not encouraged. We had a few books that we read, re-read and lent to our friends. They and Children's Hour on the wireless were our daily delight. Films, pantomime and Peter Pan in London were rare treats.'

'My childhood was spent in a village called London Colney, just south of St Albans. I was born in 1944 in a house in Napsbury Avenue and remained there until I married. For most of my childhood days it was a rough unmade road divided in the middle by white bollards, thus splitting its occupants up into two groups. Very rarely did the children from the lower end play with the children past the white bollards – "the upper end".

I have many memories of street games that we played, rounders, cricket, leapfrog, skipping, all played in the middle of the road – cars were a rarity in those days, so were no cause for concern. One thing which would interrupt our games would be the welcome bell of the ice-cream cart which was pulled along by a man on his bicycle from the nearby village of Shenley. I remember well the thin blue bubble-gum flavoured ice lollies, a real favourite amongst "our gang".

I had two older brothers so very often I was the youngest member of the gang, and sometimes hard done by. It always seemed that I was the last to be chosen when selecting teams, or the last to bat when playing rounders. My favourite game was playing sardines, especially when the evenings got dark. It was scary but exciting to go off hiding in someone's front garden, squatting behind a bush or tree in the pitch dark, breathing heavily and hoping against hope that the occupants wouldn't come out and find you. Sunday afternoons we all made our way to the top of Napsbury Avenue and there just across the road, outside Napsbury Hospital gates would be "Johnny Pedlar" with his big old brown suitcase full of interesting things which he hoped to sell to the hospital visitors, but his main audience always seemed to be our gang. He was a fascinating eccentric character and I must admit to being a bit frightened of him. He was a large man with a big nose, probably in his fifties, bald on top with long white straggly hair at the back. He always wore a black suit with waistcoat and had one of those pocket watches on a chain. He never seemed to laugh or smile but cracked many jokes and often burst into song as he was trying to sell his wares. The highlight of our visit to Johnny Pedlar would be the moment out of the blue, when he would throw a handful of sweets in the air and we would all dive to the ground hoping to find one. I remember the joy when I found a "blackjack".

Guy Fawkes night was a big event in my childhood. We had great fun making the "guy" each year and again like Johnny Pedlar would try to catch the visitors going into the hospital. With my blonde hair, blue eyes and face of innocence, I was the one made to say "A penny for the guy please".

We always had a huge bonfire in our back garden, and quite a few of our gang would be there. Hot chestnuts cooked in the bonfire with the baked potatoes were enjoyed by all. With eyes full of wonder we watched the pretty "Golden Rain", the catherine wheels whiz round, rockets ascend into the sky and moved quickly to avoid the jumping jacks tumbling menacingly around our ankles. However, there was one particular Guy Fawkes night which stands out in my memory more than all the others. That night, whilst we were in the back garden enjoying our fireworks, some boys from another gang threw a firework through our letter box, which landed on my baby sister's pram and set the blankets on fire. Fortunately my mother came indoors just in time to catch the fire before it got out of hand. I remember the distress it caused and how it dampened our spirits. We never found out exactly who the culprit was but we all had our suspicions – we only knew it was some boys from the rival gang who lived past the "white bollards".

Funnily enough I married a boy from that half of the street, although I was never aware of his existence until I was about 13, when all boys became interesting.'

OFF TO THE SWEETSHOP

'On Saturdays in the 1910s my brother and I were given pocket money to spend at old Mrs Scott's bakery shop near the Hoddesdon clock tower. Halfpenny buns, Sharps Kreemy Toffee at a penny a bar, and aniseed balls (25 for a penny) were favourites.'

'My brother and his pals would often visit our grand-mother to see if she needed any errands run, hoping to be rewarded with a halfpenny to spend on sweets or ice cream – yes, one could buy a halfpenny cornet then.

In winter the pond in Stanstead Road, Hoddesdon was frozen hard enough for us to slide on; no one could afford skates in those days.'

'Our village had one shop and it sold everything – sugar, currants, raisins, sultanas, all carefully weighed out into thick blue bags. Bags of coal and coke stood outside the shop door. Great slabs of cheese just waiting to be cut and sides of bacon, covered in muslin, hanging from the ceiling. There was always a powerful aroma of fresh ground coffee and rows and rows of glass sweet jars filled with an assortment of confections, from liquorice shoe-laces and sherbet dabs to gobstoppers and jelly babies. On Saturday mornings we would go with our penny pocket money and buy four ounces of jelly babies. We would be asked by the shopkeeper whether we wanted boys or girls, and he would advise us to have boys as there was more on them. It was years before I realised why he had given that advice.'

'When sweet rationing first ended after the Second World War (the rush necessitating sweets being rationed again) – oh, the luxury of being able to buy a packet of Polos for twopence.'

A RARE HOLIDAY

'Home life at Little Munden before the First World War was centred on working and playing together and making our own fun. When our pets died they were given a proper burial and with everything carried out correctly. Winter evenings were spent with games of tiddly winks, snakes and ladders, ludo, Happy Families, etc, with Dad and Mum joining in. Reading aloud before bedtime of *Christy's Old Organ, Jessica's First Prayer, Little Women, Jo's Boys* and only by exchanges with friends did we get a new book.

Nowadays using the car from one place to another, whether a long or short journey, is the norm, but my first sight of a car was in 1911 when the city gent bought the country house and moved in. The country folk were relying on the horse and trap, in fact every mode of travel was horse-drawn even to outings to the seaside, to the doctor in his surgery and by the clergy for church and parish visiting. The notice placed over our village shop read "Dog cart for hire" and it was by this method I was taken to the station at the age of six to be placed "In Charge of The Guard" on board a train from Charing Cross station in London, wearing my name label, for St Leonards on Sea, a great experience for a small child but I was feeling secure and quite safe. The lady in the corner seat opposite helped me to unpack my sandwiches but I gather my fingers rubbed the window many times and when Auntie met me I had to go to the washroom to be made presentable to the family. My luggage was a plaited straw dress case, with a cover which dropped over the top and a strap to hold it together. So I saw the sea for the first time.

But the annual holiday was to visit Grandfather, aunts and uncles on a hill farm in Herefordshire, which was the same excitement for each year until our school days were over. The tin trunk had to be packed and sent off "Luggage In Advance" and sure enough it was waiting for us when we arrived at the little branch line station on the borders of Radnorshire.

At Paddington we three children sat by the rest of our luggage on the platform, "as safe as houses" and never fearing that Mother would not return with the "Excursion Tickets" and a bottle of lemonade to have at lunchtime.

Life at the farm for the month of August was wonderful. We had tea with the haymakers and in cornfields watched the binders on the hilly fields. I marvelled they did not tip over. There were cows to bring in and tie up for milking, chickens and geese to be fed, pigswill to be mixed up and we looked for eggs in the most odd places. They seemed to be anywhere; some were never found but came home with mother hen as a brood of chicks.

Water was scarce and a journey for it from the river a mile away plus riding back on the waggon was a morning's outing.

Baking day came round too, when the dough was set to rise in the wooden bread trough. The fire was lit in the brick oven and a faggot of sticks was burned at one time – mainly apple wood from the orchards which we helped to collect. Cakes, apple tarts, dough cakes and bacon pies were also cooked at the same time. The delicious smell still remains with me.

Then back home until next August.'

THE BEST YEARS OF OUR LIVES?

The long walk to school, the temperamental stove which provided the only heat, silence in the classrooms – the experiences of those who went to school in the early years of the century did not differ in many respects from those of their grandchildren, particularly in small village schools. Teachers often worked minor miracles in difficult conditions, providing a basic education which has stood their pupils in good stead over the ensuing years.

GOING TO SCHOOL BEFORE THE 1920s

'Just after the turn of the century I was taken to the "Academy" (the village school at Little Munden built in 1924 by Rev John Reynolds, rector at that time) by a neighbour's daughter for my introduction to school, to be taught by "Auntie Annie". I was dressed for the occasion, for every girl had a long white pinafore with a frill over the shoulder straps. This was changed after school, trusting it was clean enough for the next day. Scripture stories, easy hymns, poetry, nursery rhymes and the three Rs were all part of the daily round.

I had a three quarter mile walk home at midday and back at half past one. The school bell might be ringing to remind us of the time as we turned the last corner. There was no playground except the road but nothing was likely to come along other than a farm horse going home with the ploughman.

I learned to knit and sew as the years passed and when the First World War came at eleven years old, we were knitting sea boot stockings for sailors, mittens and gloves

123

for soldiers overseas and sewing nightshirts for hospitals. The seniors dug a school garden from the ploughed field and provided vegetables to share round among the elderly.'

'I was born at Hertingfordbury Park on the 15th February 1905, where my father was Head Gardener. I used to help him in the vinery thinning the bunches of grapes. When I was a child I used to go with my mother gleaning after the harvest had been taken to the farm. We kept chickens. The milk was brought to the door and we took a jug for it to be put in.

I had to walk to school which was a mile and a half from

Grammar school girls at Hitchin c1920 practising their dancing. (Photograph courtesy of Hitchin Museum)

my home. There was very little traffic, mostly horse and cart, and although it was a main road it had a gravel surface. Sometimes I would take my top and spin it along the road, and other times my hoop. I had to take sandwiches for lunch, and we only had an open shelter to stand in to eat them. The school was heated with a tortoise stove. Opposite the school was a big house, which was called Lady Cowper's Training School for Girls. They were trained for domestic service. In the winter we were able to buy soup from them for a halfpenny.'

'I started school at the age of two and a half in 1913, at Well House in Green Street. This nursery school had been started for the benefit of the toddlers and young children until they were big enough to walk the mile and a half to Shenley school. It was run by the two Miss Wrights and was a very happy place. I learned all sorts of things from my ABC to numbers and knitting. After we had been home for lunch, Miss Wright would put cushions on the floor and we would all take forty winks. The charge was twopence a week.

When I was five and a half I had to go the village school in Shenley. Of course it was too far to walk home for lunch and so I had to take sandwiches. After a time a soup kitchen was set up behind the lodge house at the gates of Mr Raphael's estate (subsequently the site of Shenley hospital). I remember walking in a crocodile from the school each day for my dinner which cost twopence. These meals were lovely and beautifully cooked.

Unfortunately after about 18 months these dinners were discontinued and I had to revert to taking sandwiches. These I hated after the cooked dinners, so I used to throw them away over the hedge. Eventually I was ill and my parents found out what I had been up to. After that I was given a bicycle so that I could come home to lunch!'

'I was born in Bengeo, my father working as head gardener to McMullens Brewery Estate, West Street, Hertford. I was taken to school at the age of three by my sister before she went on to her own school in Bengeo. I remember sitting on a small chair behind a table on which was a tray filled with sand. We were given a stick and had to mark out ABC in the sand. After dancing and playing, we were given a small mat which had our name on it and we had to put this on the table before resting our heads and arms on it.

When we moved to Hertingfordbury, Father took us to Bayford school in the pony and trap. We had to walk home and were given permission to walk through the Brickendon Bury Park estate. As our headmaster was Welsh, we had a very good choir and won many trophies. I also sang at the old Crystal Palace.

We moved again, this time to Harmers Green. We had to walk to school in Digswell and once a week we walked over to the Warren (two miles each way) for extra lessons, held in the old tin hall.'

GETTING THERE

'I still live in the same house at Welham Green that my father built at the turn of the century before he was married. We had no railway station or buses when I was a child in the 1910s, so we had to walk to Potters Bar or Hatfield to get a train. It was usually Potters Bar, where we walked along the cinder path by the side of the railway.

We also had quite a walk to school at Waterend. In the summertime we walked across the fields to school, but in winter we had to keep to the roads, as the swallow holes at the back of the school were flooded and the water rushed under Kettle Bridge nearby. On wet days, the school had slippers and socks for us to change into and hot cocoa was made for us on the round coke stove in the classroom.'

'I lived in a small hamlet called Cherry Green, which consisted of five other houses and a farm. Our nearest village was Westmill, which was about a mile and half away. Our water came from a well on the green, our milk from the farm was threepence per pint and our eggs were free.

To go to school, I went in a farm cart pulled by a horse called Stanley. If that failed to turn up, as so often happened, then myself and five other children had to walk. On cold winter days we would all take some cocoa powder and sugar in an Oxo tin. Our teacher would then make us a cup of hot cocoa, which went down very well. During the spring and summer, about every six weeks, a man would be outside the school gates with a big suitcase full of lovely things like pencils, paints, books, marbles, sweets and much more. These could be exchanged for quite good secondhand clothes, the better the clothes the better the present – this to a five year old was magic!

On walking back home from school across the fields I would often see my grandfather having a well earned rest from hedge laying or scything. He would share his bottle of cold tea and bread and cheese with me. I wasn't allowed tea at home so this was a special treat for me – only grandad and myself knew about it.

One of the best things for me in those days was going down to the farm at weekends to help with the milking, grinding up the cow cake or helping to pick and store the apples. I don't know if I was in anyone's way or not but nothing was ever said. The farm employed about 18 men and they all seemed very contented in their work. I wish I still had the corn dollies that were made by some of the ladies as we sat watching the corn being cut on a lovely warm autumn day.'

'In 1937, when I was five, I lived in Berkhamsted on the borders of Northchurch. My earliest memory of life at Park View Road school was the dark stone-floored cloakroom where at the row of white wash basins we had to gargle twice daily with salt water because of the outbreak of diphtheria in the area and this was a killer.

At the tender age of five, I and two friends walked two to two and a half miles to school, home for "dinner" at noon, back to school at 1.30 and home again at 4pm. A total of eight miles at least every day. This went on until I was eight when we shortened the distance by going over the lockgates of the canal and along the towpath. The horses pulling some of the barges used to frighten us and so did the herd of cows in the field we had to traverse. The cows always gathered round the gate, but the most dangerous encounter was with the metal trucks pulled by a horse taking coal from the trucks on the railway, under a tunnel we had to go through and along to the gas works beside the canal. If we got into the tunnel under the railway when the horse and trucks arrived we had to run for our lives.'

SCHOOL BETWEEN THE WARS

'We lived on a farm at Kentish Lane between Essendon and Brookmans Park from 1917 to 1922. We walked to Westfield school every day, living much closer than those children who walked from Wild Hill and Bell Barr. The large schoolroom was divided into two by a curtain. On one side sat the older children up to 14 years of age and on the other were those from seven years. The infants were in a separate room. In the wintertime the headmaster provided us with hot cocoa.

When I was eleven I won a scholarship and every Monday I was taken by pony and trap to Cole Green station to catch the train to Hertford. Then I walked along the track to Hertford East to catch the train to Ware and the grammar school. I spent Monday to Friday in lodgings and returned by train on Friday to Cole Green, and then walked back to Kentish Lane. On one occasion my boots fell to pieces!'

'Our girls school at Hatfield in the 1920s was known as The Old Girls or London Road School. What happy memories I have of my short time there. It was a revelation after the strict routine of a large London school, where there were 60 in my class. Our room here was heated by a large tortoise stove and it was one of my joys to take turns in stoking it. This meant climbing out of the window – it was a one storey school – and filling the hod from a huge pile of coke dumped in a corner of the playground. This we had to smash with a coke-sledge hammer first, then haul it ourselves back through the classroom window.

Our teacher was Miss Lambert – "Cis" to us behind her back – but I did so love her. We became friends for many years after my school days.

The headmistress was Miss Carter. She rode to school on a large three wheeled cycle dressed in voluminous black, for all the world looking like Queen Victoria, but for all her stern, majestic appearance she was a most kind lady.

I was walking down the flight of steps known as Jacobs Ladder when I saw the then Marchioness of Salisbury on her way to our school. She came each year to present prizes to the domestic science pupils. She told us she preferred to walk down from Hatfield House. Our domestic teacher Miss Hirons, had instructed us thoroughly in the manner in which we had to hold our skirts or pinnies and bob and curtsy before her ladyship on receiving our prizes with a clear "Thank you my Lady". Every girl received a little gift from her – it was a bun and an orange! A treat in those days. I was astonished to know I had won the housewifery prize and received a writing case from her, plus my bun and orange.'

'We went to school from four to fourteen years old; the boys went on to school in Hertford, the girls had to leave and get a job. Our village school stood close to the centre of Bayford and the "old school house" where the head-master lived stood next door. We had three classrooms, three teachers, about 80 children and earth closets! How did we manage? At lunch time we were taken up to the village hall where a meal had been cooked for us. Our playground was strictly segregated, no mixing with boys even at that early age. We had coal fires in the classrooms and a stove in winter where we tried to thaw our frozen bottles of milk. The school owned a small allotment where once a week the boys were taught how to grow veget-ables. We girls stayed in school to embroider, sew knick-ers or dusters, and knit.'

'The boys and girls at Abbots Langley had separate schools, and the toilets had a back flap for bucket emptying. The little horrors of boys would creep behind the girls' toilets with stinging nettles, carefully held with a hanky wound round the stem, and torment the girls. It is to be hoped that the hardy village girls were able to get their own back.'

'I went to school at Baas Hill on the Broxbournebury estate. I walked there across Grass Norris (where Cardinal Bourne school was later built), which in winter was too boggy to cross, and on through the woods. It was a long walk for a five year old. Most of the girls wore pinafores to school but my mother wouldn't let me. At eleven I transferred to Ware grammar school as a paying pupil because the Baas Hill headmistress didn't believe in scholarships and wouldn't let her girls take the exam. I travelled there on a yellow open-topped solid-tyred "boneshaker" school bus under strict instructions from Miss Brough of the grammar school that there was to be no fraternisation whatsoever with the boys travelling to Hertford grammar school!'

'The girls and infants school in our village was about a one and a half mile walk to the top of Baas Hill. The building was a beautiful red brick, two-roomed place with the school house adjoining. A stone plaque on the wall said – "This school was erected in the year 1867 as a memorial to the late George Jacob Bosanquet Esq of Broxbournebury by his widow."

The larger room was used for eight to 14 year olds and the smaller room for five to seven year olds and both were heated by a combustion stove. Nearby is the original Elizabethan manor house and beyond the garden, known as "The Springs". It was a great joy to us to have our lunch in the Springs by the pond and build "houses" in the bracken. Time just flew and we seldom heard the whistle!

After I had been at school for a year, the two teachers left and new ones came. This is a daunting time for small children, but what a really marvellous change – we went from Victorian times to a completely new era. Firstly, the old forms were removed and new pine tables and chairs took their place. We sat two at a table and my table was joined up to another table and we were called "Stove Square". Instead of slates, we had pads and notebooks. We used the method of "Choice" – the Montessori method. Having done the work set for a period, it was put into covers which we designed and sent to be marked. This method was frowned upon by the local powers, but we continued!

Handiwork played a large part with pottery, leather work, raffia and canework, and drama – a great joy. This I really loved. One summer we were doing "Hiawatha". Then the blow fell – I had chicken pox and was away for three weeks and when I came back – horrors – the set was ready on the front lawn; even the wigwam was in place. Not for me the poignant cry "Gitche Maniti the Mighty – give your children food, O Father" – I was devastated. At Christmas we had a wonderful party which meant going home in the dark – a thing not to be thought of these days.

During this time, a new school was being built in the village and in 1931 we all departed and left our lovely old school with very mixed feelings after so many happy years.'

'All the children at Redbourn walked to school, some across rough fields, and as there were no school dinners, many went home again at lunchtime. Milk was provided in school in one third pint bottles with cardboard lids which were collected and strung across the garden as bird scarers. In winter, the milk was often frozen and was put in front of the classroom fire to thaw. There was no other heat so children sitting near the fire scorched while those a few feet away froze. A thoughtful teacher would move her pupils around.'

'Our family went to Tewin Cowper Endowed School and had to walk, no school buses in those days. In the cold weather, we would carry a hot baked potato to school to keep our hands warm and eat it when we got there. No hot school dinners, except on the day the girls had a cookery lesson. Generally speaking it was jam sand-

School milk was a regular part of every schoolchild's day, even when it had to be defrosted in the winter! (Photograph courtesy of Hitchin Museum)

wiches for lunch. The boys did gardening and looked after the bees. The rainfall was also taken every day. Every year we were given a party alternatively by the British Legion and WI. These parties were really appreciated, we played games like musical chairs and the food was lovely. Another treat the school had was a visit to Panshanger House, by invitation of Lord and Lady Desborough. We walked from Tewin across the fields to Panshanger. Big white sheets were laid all over the floors and carpets. We were given a lovely tea party and then a magic lantern show, then shown round the vast kitchen. I can still see in my mind the huge number of pots and pans, all gleaming, round the wall and on the shelves, but above all the huge bells all round the top of the wall with room numbers under them. Races were held in the Park and one of the races was from a given point to the "Big Oak" and back. We received an apple and orange on leaving.

On our way home from school, Mr Hopkyns would be standing at his orchard gate and give us apples which were eaten before we got home. Sometimes he gave us "dropped" cookers to take home.'

'At the age of eleven, my family moved from North London to Bovingdon and I started school at Berkhamsted School for Girls. I caught the train from what was then called Boxmoor station, and each day I walked the distance of a mile and a half to this station (because it was good for me – so my mother said), and each day I passed a notice at the top of the steep hill which read: "Every driver who injures the roadway by descending the hill with a locked wheel which has not a properly adjusted skidpan will be prosecuted." There were about 40 girls using the train to Berkhamsted. They came from Bushey, Watford, Kings Langley and Boxmoor and in the other direction from Tring and Cheddington. Boys from Berkhamsted Boys School also used the train, but we were not allowed to speak to them. We had special "Ladies Only" compartments reserved for us, but we found that if one leant out of the window far enough and one's boy friend in the next compartment did the same, notes could be passed!

When we arrived at Berkhamsted we had to form two crocodiles – the Senior Croc and the Junior Croc with two prefects or senior girls in charge of each. We walked in the roadway so as not to block the footpath for other pedestrians (there was not much traffic in those days). We wore straw boaters summer and winter, dark green gym slips with white blouses (gym slip must be four inches from the ground when kneeling), black stockings and navy costumes for more formal occasions and thick navy coats in winter. Latterly we were allowed green cotton dresses in summer and green blazers.

We were all rather amused by the notice on the inside of each toilet door which read: "It is important that every girl should strive to obtain daily action of the bowels. The only way to ensure this is to visit the WC at the same time every day, the best time being immediately after breakfast."'

'Secondary school days in the 1930s were most enjoyable and quite a challenge. There was daily travel some ten miles by train to attend the nearest grammar school, including Saturday mornings for obligatory games. Only pupils travelling a certain distance by train or bus were provided with hot dinners at a small charge, one cook providing between 20 to 30 superb meals. Dinnertime was a ritual; the duty teacher was entrusted to carve a large joint of meat on Mondays, another day there might be toad in the hole, shepherds pie, liver and bacon or fish. Duty monitors served the vegetables and gravy. All plates had to be emptied before the sweet course could be served. The standard of food was high. Bad luck if you did not like anything as there was no choice. At the end of the day anyone could stay on for another hour or so to do supervised homework, sustained by a sticky currant bun and a drink at a small charge.

Winter uniform was worn from September regardless of an Indian Summer! This consisted of a navy blue melton cloth overcoat frequently with a half belt at the back, navy velour hat with badge and ribbon band, lisle stockings and black shoes, a navy blue gym tunic, white blouse, tie and navy pullover with lightweight black indoor shoes.

From Easter onwards the uniform was either a blue or green cotton gingham dress, panama hat, white socks, sandals and white gloves and blazer. To be seen in the town without wearing your hat was almost a mortal sin.'

'I spent most of my learning days at a school in Hemel Hempstead. The building was an old rambling house which catered for a few boarders as well as day pupils. All lessons were taught by the headmistress, a very gaunt and upright lady in a large, lofty and cold room. In winter there was a blazing coal fire and you either froze or roasted in class depending where you sat. Silence had to be observed at all times unless questions were asked about work. Meals were taken in a large dining room, where once again silence and impeccable manners were the order of the day. We had to sit bolt upright at table as leaning over was bad for our posture. If we stayed for tea, the choice of food was bread and marg or bread and jam, usually a slice of each, and cake was only on the table once a week and then only of the plainest variety.

Washing for the boarders was done in an outhouse with an enormous steaming copper and iron mangle. The clothes were plunged up and down with a wooden copper stick, first being scrubbed on a washboard to remove the dirt. All the work in the wash-house was done by an ancient housekeeper who could easily have walked out of the pages of a Dickens story book. She was dressed entirely in black with a mob cap and starched apron.

Sporting activities were minimal, but we used to go walking in an orderly crocodile. All the vegetables for the school were grown by an old gardener who was also the commissionaire at the local cinema! His favourite vegetable was Jerusalem Artichokes which he grew in abundance, because he thought they were beneficial to our diet. Needless to say, they were not the particular flavour of the day, as most of us hated them, myself included.'

'I began at Hunton Bridge school in January in the early 1930s, and remember the roaring coal fire and the high fire-guard we stood by to read to teacher. The back of the schoolroom was cold, and the outside toilets even colder and often frozen.

At least the infants had their own schoolroom, as juniors and seniors shared one lofty room also with one fire! Here infants and junior mistresses baked their lunch potato in the ashes. The headmaster lived in the school-house.

Only a few farm children stayed to sandwich lunches, as they walked several miles in all weathers, some across fields and others through long winding lanes. We in the village or those who lived in newer roads walked home to cooked dinners, as mothers all stayed at home and had no outside jobs.

The tea time journeys home we'd play seasonal games, marbles, skipping, ball, and snowballing with scant traffic worries. We would cluster round the doorway of the blacksmith's forge if any farm horses were being shod, to hear the anvil ring with hammers as the iron shoes were made, and watch the hot shoes skilfully fitted – then hissing in the water, cooled and nailed to the huge hooves.'

THROUGH THE WAR AND AFTER

'When I was at infants school (Gravley School, Tring) we were kept warm in winter with a big black, round, closed-in fire in the middle of class. We all sat round it to warm our hands. We learnt to write our names on wooden-framed slates with chalk. I can remember learning to do French knitting, on a wooden cotton reel with four nails knocked in it, and then it was sewn into round table mats. We also made pom-poms with milk bottle cardboard tops we saved. This was in the 1940s.'

'I remember trips to St Albans on Saints days and feast days from my senior school, Townsend Church of England. We used to walk there and back every day from home, no mention of getting a bus in those days. When I first started school at Townsend one side was for boys and the other for girls, and we shared the school hall for services and PT (Physical Training). There wasn't room even in those days for the first form, we had to troop down to St Michael's Memorial Hall in Branch Road (where the Express Dairy was, and still is – at least that's one thing that hasn't changed). However the Memorial Hall was great fun because we had this enormous building (well, it appeared so then) all to ourselves, with fields all around (no road to Hemel Hempstead then). We used to try to get through the fence at the back and go down to the river Ver to catch tiddlers – the spankings we used to get once we got home for having wet shoes and socks.

They were happy days, despite the war. We had two late summer times, so it never got dark until about 11 pm, (mind you, I wasn't allowed to stay up so late), but it was a special treat to walk down to Warwicks for a tuppenny bag of chips, and eat them on the way home.'

'September 5th 1939 was hardly the happiest day to be starting secondary school, but with other new girls, very obvious in our brand new oversized blazers and navy velour hats, I set out for Ware Grammar School for my first day. We were expected to have with us the paraphernalia required for games and PT, geometry sets and pencil cases etc. We then received a letter from the headmistress asking that each girl should have extra clothing in case we had to go into the underground air raid shelters and something to protect our heads. My head protector was an enamel washing up bowl, thankfully I never had to wear it. How could we forget the ever present gas mask too?

138

It was clear that this amount of gear would not fit into a briefcase or satchel and I approached my new school carrying a kit bag, travelling on a 310 bus. The windows of all the buses had been covered with a net meshing stuck to the glass to give some protection from glass splinters and we peered through a postcard size piece of clear glass to see where we were. Inevitably the net meshing was picked at and pulled away from the glass, causing little official notices to appear from "Billy Brown of London Town" which read "I trust you'll pardon my correction – That stuff is there for your protection."

The buildings of the school were a hotch-potch of old houses joined to a newer building of classrooms, laboratory, assembly hall and an outdoor gymnasium. The school could just about cope with the number of pupils, but to our surprise when fears of the Blitz began we shared the buildings with girls and teachers from Hastings High School and a convent school from Holloway. Such severe overcrowding was intolerable and for some time the classrooms were used on a rota system of mornings and afternoons with games and PT to complete the timetable.

There was no central heating in the school, each classroom was heated by small gas radiators which were only lit when we arrived in the mornings, but it seemed that the gas flames were so feeble that it was mid-day before we could feel any warmth from them and on cold days we often started our lessons wearing overcoats.

As the months passed a more normal school routine was established although cookery classes were very limited in what we could achieve due to strict rationing of basic ingredients. There was a shortage of paper too, before a new book was issued the old one had to be examined by a teacher and signed to say that every available space had been used.

The school adopted a Royal Navy ship and we knitted

balaclava helmets, scarves, socks and mittens for the crew.

At last one afternoon, I was walking past the study of Miss H Woodhead, the headmistress, when she flung open the door and shouted to me "The war is going to end tomorrow." The next day, 8th May, was a holiday for everyone. I spent the day with my friends rowing on the Lea at Broxbourne. We heard an aeroplane overhead and for the first time we realised it could only be "one of ours" and that the threat from the sky was really over. Less than a week later I left school to start my first job in London.'

'I went to school at Abbots Langley church school and used to walk there and back from Leavesden, staying at school for dinner (which most of us disliked intensely). We had coal fires with a large guard round them, on which the teachers used to perch, keeping the fire from the children. In winter it was terribly cold and the free bottles of milk were often frozen and put in front of the fires to try to thaw them in time for "play time".

I joined the local Brownie pack and also walked there on my own and came back in the dark. It was quite safe and I realise now what a wonderful time it was, and what a shame it will never be the same again.

We had lessons on cookery one week and laundry the following week. These were held at Kings Langley school, and of course we walked there and back. I remember enjoying these walks, especially dawdling along the canal towpath.'

'My school memories are very clear. Do we ever forget that first day when our mothers leave us at the school door with a stranger and then disappear? It came as a shock to realise that I was expected to go every week-day and not just when I felt like it. My earliest battle with my teacher was over the compulsory milk we had at morning break. It came in a third of a pint bottle, freezing cold in winter and lukewarm in summer; the cardboard top had a hole in the centre which had to be pierced to insert a straw. Ugh! How I hated milk and did everything I could to avoid drinking it. The cardboard tops were saved and we had to work wool up through the centre hole and over the edge until the top was completely covered; these circles were then joined to make mats.

Hands up all those who remember Empire Day! On 24th May we went to school in the morning dressed in red, white and blue, and sang patriotic songs in the playground, waving our little Union Jacks on sticks, but the afternoon was a holiday. The games in the playground had their seasons – spinning tops, hoops, marbles, intricate skipping routines and various ball games. No one ever said "Next week let's all change to marbles or whatever", it just seemed to happen. We used to decorate our tops with coloured or silver paper which made lovely effects as the tops were spinning. Two of the teachers looked positively ancient to me and I found out later that my father and several aunts had also been taught by these same ladies. It was a gentle schooling at Oxhey Junior School, the worst thing I can remember happening was running along a corridor from the classroom (strictly forbidden!), and falling flat on my back which completely winded me and frightened me so much I never did run inside the school again.

Progressing to London Road Senior School, which had a specially built Domestic Centre, the girls were expected to learn basic skills which would fit us for the time when we became wives. Starting with needlework, we learned the correct way to do seams, hems and darning, then the more proficient were allowed to use the two sewing machines available, and by the end of the term we had to have made our own apron in readiness for when we started our laundry course at the centre, this in turn was

141

followed by housewifery and finally cookery. A Miss Pine was the awe-inspiring head of this department, to us a real dragon and so strict. At the end of the practical part of each session, we had to make notes in an exercise book, and I can remember what a stickler she was for spelling, not my best subject, so I rarely got ten out of ten. Even a blot or missing comma lost marks. I still have this notebook and in November 1942 the recipe was "Wartime Short Crust Pastry" using 4 oz flour, 2 oz fine oatmeal, 2 oz margarine and cooking fat, plus one teaspoon of baking powder, pinch of salt and cold water. One very embarrassing memory comes to mind during my cookery course. As it was wartime, a condition of our school being provided with foodstuffs to enable our lessons to continue was that we had to cook lunches and sell these to local evacuees who came to the centre. On this particular occasion I was serving soup and ended up tipping the whole lot in one unfortunate lady's lap. After that I was given the job of selling tickets at the door, where it was probably felt I could do less damage.

Now came another change of schools, this time to a private one in Stanmore, but because the bombing in that area got so bad, it was decided to close the school early for the summer break. I was 14 years old and my schooling came to an abrupt end.'

'In the autumn in the late 1940s it was back to school, a tiny primary school at Hinxworth with two classrooms, one for children aged between five and seven and the other for older children of eight to eleven years. In the older children's classroom was a large "tortoise" stove which was filled each morning with coke by the part-time caretaker. If the wind was in the wrong direction it let out steady puffs of smoke and fumes and the windows had to be opened whatever the weather. If the wind was right it burnt merrily away, sending out a warm glow, which

142

made us all very reluctant to go into the playground at milk break (a third of a pint given to each child).

We all lined up on Friday mornings to be given a dessertspoonful of cod liver oil and malt. Once out in the playground we chased around to keep warm playing "Tag", "Statues" and when we got older "Kiss Chase" – the boys chased the girls and when they caught them tried to kiss them. Needless to say the girls learnt to run very fast to avoid the boys. After the bell went we all rushed back inside out of the cold to wrestle with the complexities of Reading, Writing and Arithmetic.

Each day from 3 to 3.45 we had a story from a book chosen by the teacher, each pupil reading a page, and we were always sad when the story was finished or the bell went and we had to go home. On cold days to be huddled around the stove was glorious.'

'I was brought up in "border country", the border, that is, between Hertfordshire and Essex. At the age of eleven in 1955, this border existence became official when I started school at the Hertfordshire and Essex High School in Bishop's Stortford.

That first day is easy to recall; not in detail but in remembered sensations. Perhaps the keenest is the smell of new uniform. Not only was it crisp and heavy, but the colour! Dark brown, a colour that made an eleven year old feel very grown up. We wore a tie to indicate which house we were in and my scarlet one made me think more of cut throats than anything else.

I was at the Herts & Essex when it celebrated its Golden Jubilee in 1960. On 25th May, the whole school dressed properly in full school uniform, including berets or hats, walked in crocodile form by form the mile and a half across the town to St Michael's church. I was in the choir so we left earlier than the rest of the school for a rehearsal. The preacher was the Bishop of Bedford, but the thing I remember most vividly was the anthem *Praise God in His Holiness* by Armstrong Gibbs. It was new and exciting and the thrill of the sound we made is still with me. You don't forget the first experience of that kind.'

THE WORLD OF WORK

HOW WE MADE A LIVING

Having left school, what kind of opportunities for making a living were open to the men and women of the past? Paper making, watercress picking, engineering, corset making, are just a few of the jobs we remember.

FROM CORSETS TO JAM

'My father came from an Oxhey/Bushey family. Grandfather was a lime burner, living in a house at the lime kilns then situated near Bushey Arches.'

'I left school at 14 in 1921 and got a job as an additional help at a shop in Shenley. In the mornings I helped a Mrs Smith with housework. One day when we did the bedrooms we found a sixpence under the dressing table. Mrs Smith was not only older than I was, she was much more outspoken. "I reckon she had put that there to see if we move the furniture out," said Mrs Smith. "That's the last time she does that!" I don't know exactly what was said, but we never found any more money after that. In the afternoon I was told to bind the mats. My poor fingers. I could hardly get the needle in it was so hard. When my employer came home from her teaching job at the boys' school, I was ticked off for not having done much – and there I was nearly crying with the pain in my fingers. All this for five shillings a week.

In 1923 a vacancy occurred for a monitress at the Shenley school and along with several other hopefuls I applied. I think I was selected because I was able to play the piano a bit. This was a much better paid job – about £7 a month.'

146

'Before the First World War there was only one employer in Baldock – the brewery. Everyone was connected with it in some way or another. Local deliveries were made by horse until 1940 and later, deliveries at a slightly further distance were made by a magnificent steam dray.

My father did carting for local contractors when money was short and there was not enough work for the horses on the farm. It was fun to sit up there with him or to clamber onto my uncle's bakery van and kick my school friends off while claiming proprietorship.

In the 1920s a new employer came to Baldock – a stocking factory known locally as "the factory", "the Fulfa" or "the Bondor". Suddenly all the girls who would have had to go into service for a pittance found a new well paid job. Workers were brought in from Nottinghamshire and Leicestershire and new accents came to Baldock. Those second generation accents still persist to this day.'

'In 1925 we moved to Welwyn Garden City where my father obtained work helping to build the Shredded Wheat factory and the Welwyn Theatre (no longer in existence). When this work was finished he was employed by the council in the roadworks department.

When I was 14 I started my first job at Barclays Corsets factory. I was employed as a machinist on corsetry using an electric machine. My working hours were from eight to five, with one week's holiday a year.

The war started and I was called up to do war work in a factory called Norton Grinding Wheels, using an electric handsaw. I also worked in the Kiln Department, the end product being emery stones and emery wheels to be used in various industries. My hours were shifts of six o'clock to two one week and two to ten the second week.'

'The Spirella corset factory employed over a thousand women at Letchworth. The garments were all made to measure and orders were sent from all over the country by lady corsetieres who were trained in the factory, termed as "schools". There would be a hundred or two at any one time, and they would be lodged out all over town while training. Cleanliness was important and there were hot baths for those who did not have baths at home.'

'Some folk at Redbourn cycled to work outside the village or travelled by workman's bus to Apsley paper mills, but there was employment in the village at the jam factory, the silk mill or the tan yard – where the smell was notorious. There was work for brickies and carpenters and on the farms as hedgers, ditchers and thatchers.'

'Abbots Langley was a country village in the 1930s but industry provided work for many local people. Paper mills and the Ovaltine factory in the Gade valley, and Odham's Press in Watford all needed hundreds of workers. Leavesden Hospital, "The Asylum", was where many people worked, caring for mentally frail Londoners behind mighty yellow brick walls and long barred windows. Some people commuted to London jobs. Village women were employed as maids and some families had gardeners, working several days a week.'

'On leaving school at 14 in 1931, my first job in Watford was at the Sun Engraving in the proofreading room. This was followed for a while by work at John Dickinson's. Later I returned to Sun Engraving, working first in the machine room, then in the warehouse. The starting wage was twelve shillings and sixpence a week, rising to 30 shillings. Hours were eight to six o'clock, with two ten minute breaks and an hour for lunch. This was considered a well paid job. On piecework we could often double the weekly wage, and go home on Fridays feeling very rich.'

'I started work at a small light engineering factory called Vanderveriens at Little Gaddesden, several of us used to cycle there and back from Berkhamsted. It's not there now. After that I learnt to become a paper-bag machine operator at John Dickinson's in the Packing Supplies Department. I used to travel on the Apsley Mills bus from Potten End and I met my future husband there at the mill, he was my printer.

Both of my grandfathers worked on the Ashridge Estate; one was a gamekeeper, the other an agricultural worker who did layering of hedges, shepherding etc. My father was a gardener all his working life, and during the war he worked in the cornfields when he was home on leave. I remember him bringing home a day old rabbit in his pocket, and Mum fed it from a fountain pen filler. It grew up indoors and played up and down the stairs with the cat.'

'My father worked on the LNER based at Hitchin, first as a fireman on the steam locomotives, and eventually as a driver of the steam locomotive, mostly taking the trains from Hitchin to Kings Cross and back and from Hitchin to Cambridge and back. He would often take food with him in an enamel dish (probably bacon and eggs or something similar) which would be put on the coal shovel and lodged on the fire in the engine to be cooked as they were travelling along.'

DRESSMAKING AND MILLINERY

'At the tender age of eleven years, my mother left school and continued her education in real life by entering an apprenticeship to dressmaking. Very long hours were worked for a very small wage. Several girls worked together in a local prestigious dressmaking establishment. Such intricacies as gathering, pleating and tucking on beautiful materials were learned. Special occasion dresses were made for the ladies of the district, also elaborate wedding gowns. There were no days off except for very special occasions and rules were very strict. Her few leisure hours were spent mainly with chapel activities. Much interest was shown to my mother by the choir-master who greatly encouraged her many musical talents. Under his tuition she learned to play the piano, organ and mandolin and become a contralto singer and in conse-quence she entertained at local concerts.'

'My father wanted me to have a little hat shop when I grew up, so in 1936 when I left school at the age of 14, I was sent to a work-room attached to the millinery depart-ment in a smart ladies' outfitters in Hitchin. As I was on trial, I received three shillings and sixpence: having no purse I put this princely sum in my pocket, but when I arrived home all I discovered was a hole in the pocket. After the first week my wages were increased to seven and sixpence.

I worked in a long, narrow room with a long table, a treadle sewing machine, a few wooden head-shapes cal-led 'blocks' and a steam kettle, with Miss Fleming, the milliner at one end and me at the other.

The fashionable young ladies from the show-room would bring a hat to be altered or retrimmed or even made smaller. Miss Fleming would arrange the new rib-bon or feathers and veiling and then hand it to me clamped between finger and thumb for me to stitch, but no stitches showing!

Some customers would bring a blurred photograph out of the Tatler of someone wearing a hat they wanted copied in the colour of their choice. Perhaps it would be of felt or silk to match a dress.

I loved being sent to our wonderful ribbon and trim-ming department to find ribbons, feather pads or quills and real silk to match to sew with. It took me twelve months of learning how to make a knot by rolling the thread between my fingers, how to cut strips of velvet on the bias for making hats smaller, to making a stiff brimmed 'titfer' by myself, probably for some bride's mother.

My father's dream of a hat shop for me was never to materialize as in 1939, the outbreak of war meant my brother was called up and I had to take his place working in my father's shoe shop in Hertford.'

TEA AND WATERCRESS

'I lived with my Granny at Sarratt Bottom; she worked at the watercress beds on the river Chess, pulling and tying bunches of cress. The latest baby would be taken along and lain in a "flat" watercress basket. The watercress was taken by horse and cart to Chalfont Road station and thence to Covent Garden. Granny's hands were always twisted due to the work in cold water.'

'There were plenty of watercress beds in the little rivers around Hemel Hempstead and people found part time work there in the season.'

'From the beginning of the war until the early 1950s, my parents had their own tea gardens at Waterford. Everything was home produced and my father also collected watercress from the local rivers for their "famous" watercress teas. Sunday was the busiest day; cycling clubs, mostly from North London, would come in from 6 am for early cups of tea before doing a 25 mile race to Stevenage and back. They would then return for a cooked breakfast. Roast lunches were served to more cycling clubs and hikers (sometimes 40 to 60 arriving together) and then watercress teas from 3 pm onwards. My sister and I were employed between church services and Sunday school, serving food, washing and wiping up (with no hot water apart from that heated up in the electric copper) and still no sanitation.

Monday was another extremely busy day for Mum. All the tables were covered by crisp white starched table-cloths, so the copper was in use again, together with a large bath of soapy water, a scrubbing board and brush and the famous Reckitts blue bag. Not forgetting the very big mangle. In the evening my sister and I had to help with the ironing. There was also of course, all the family's clothing.'

THE POST OFFICE

'During the Second World War I worked at Stevenage post office as an S C & T officer (Sorting, Central & Telegram Officer) in charge of the sorting office, where eight postmen and two postwomen were employed.

My hours of duty were 4.50am to 1.10pm, one week, followed by the 1.10pm to 10.00pm duty with an hour and a half tea break. As I held the keys to the office it was important that I never arrived late. In retrospect how did I dare cycle three miles in the blackout at 19 years of age?

My duties were to receive the mail collected from the railway station by a postman, and record registered mail etc. Once the postmen were out on their "walks" I was kept busy sorting all the incoming mail, which was first franked by hand, then sorted into pigeonholes and each bundle tied with string, then put into the appropriate bag for dispatch. This task was frequently interrupted by the sending and receiving of telegrams, and should a tele-gram need to wait more than five minutes after it came up the shute from the counter, I had to stop to write an excuse on the back, usually "dispatching mail". I recall with sadness still, the two telegrams I received which started with the dreaded words, "It is with deep regret that we have to inform you that your son did not return

152

A cheery word from the postwoman was a good way to start the day at Hexton in the 1940s. (Photograph courtesy of Hitchin Museum)

from operations over Germany last night." I still recall the names of those two young men, one of whom I knew.

I also dealt with "dead letters", paid wages and when on late duty, my last job was to balance the cash account. At about 9pm I'd go down to the front office and, perched on a high stool, set about balancing the books. When the books didn't balance the messenger boy, whose job it was to take the books in to the postmaster each morning, would when possible cycle over to tell me, "Don't worry the mistake wasn't yours, so-and-so had made a mistake." She would then be called in to the postmaster's office and be reprimanded.

The postmaster, an extremely severe character, and his family lived over the shop as it were, and on Christmas Day 1944 I was on duty, and to my surprise was invited up for breakfast. Yes in those days there was a Christmas Day delivery. What was unusual about my job? The postmaster returning from a meeting one day told me he had discovered I was the only female in the county doing this job, and possibly the only one in the country.'

NOT SO BAD AFTER ALL

'In January 1936 I had left school at 14 and started my first job in the office of a local paper company. Quite suddenly in those early days of January we were mourning the death of our monarch – King George V. The day of the funeral came and everybody stayed at home to listen to the service on the wireless, but to me it was a day of great relief because I had found, to my horror, that I hated the grown up world of commercialism.

The indignity of not being allowed a cup of tea from the trolley as it passed through the office, of having to work overtime until eight o'clock at night for which I received a thin slice of ham with bread and butter, and worst of all standing in the office trying to explain that the conversation I had with a colleague really was about work! Then one day I was wandering along the road dreading the return to that slide rule sitting on my desk, when I heard the slow trudge of men's feet and into view came the Hunger Marchers from Jarrow – 200 thin, ill-nourished, bedraggled, unemployed men walking the 295 miles from their hometown to London.

I returned to my desk – I didn't like work any better, but the sight of that walking depression helped me to grow up on the wet and windy day.'

ON THE FARM

Agriculture was by far the largest employer in the county, as it always had been, but things began to change during the first half of the century. Where sons had followed father into farm work, now they had the opportunity to take on factory work or to travel further afield in search of better paid or more congenial employment. Farmwork itself changed too, as the working horse gradually disappeared from the fields and mechanisation took over.

HORSES TO TRACTORS

'I live on Moor Green, about a mile from Ardeley, and my neighbour, an old farmer who died aged 95 about two years ago, used to tell me about the old days. He said they paid men £5 for a month's work during the harvest, £1 for each week and £1 bonus at the end. Teams of two horses, each team looked after by a horsekeeper, were originally used to pull the ploughs, until tractors came in. Before the advent of the combine harvester, the wheat and barley used to be gathered in sheaves, set in stooks and then into stacks. Most of the corn was put into sacks to be collected by lorry, the sacks weighing about 18 stone each, whereas nowadays the grain goes straight off in the lorries.'

'I was born in Hitchin and my father was a stallion walker. This meant he took the stallion around the farms to service the mares.'

'Most of the men at Bovingdon early in the century worked on the farm, and a cart would take eggs and straw to London and return with soot which the farmer used to fertilise his fields. At Christmas they would take holly, going one day and returning the next.'

'The local farms at Hunton Bridge were to play a large part in my life as the school I moved to had a wartime Rabbit Club and later on a school goat and her subsequent kid. This led me on to work with goats and poultry at 14, and ultimately in 1947 with cows, where my first task was to fetch the herd plus bull in at milking time!

At this small old-fashioned farm, we would sit hand milking the huge animals at 6 am by the soft light of oil lamps on whitewashed wooden walls. In a snowy winter which it seemed would never end, we'd shiver in the doorless dairy as we washed buckets in cold water, and fed the farm cats.

Spring finally came, and we sang a tune which became associated with Princess Elizabeth and Prince Philip, *People will say we're in love* from the musical *Oklahoma*. Calves frisked, and June found we two girls helping load the sweet smelling hay onto horse wagons with pitchforks, then trying our hand at rick-building. ("Keep the centre up, girls.")

On my next farm, the head carter allowed me to build my own hay stack, as he called instructions from where he loaded the pony-driven hay elevator, which kept me inundated with tangled mounds of hay. This was brought to the site by two horses with a wide wooden hay sweep between them.

My stack was eventually thatched, and stood rock firm all winter, and I hated the day when we had finished cutting the old stack with the heavy iron hayknife, and my rick was opened!

On both these farms we hand stooked all the corn sheaves in neat rows to dry thoroughly after the corn was cut with the clattering horse binder. The first swath round each field was scythed and the sheaves hand-tied with a straw twist to allow space for the horses to walk without damaging the standing corn. As the corn square grew smaller rabbits would bolt out, with fast running boys or dogs after them! Once dry the sheaves were also built into

Stooking corn by hand at Abbots Langley in the 1950s.

ricks and thatched. As autumn turned to winter, the huge threshing machine would trundle up the farm road, pulled by a hissing smoke-belching steam engine, and the filthy work of threshing corn began.

All the farm men wore string tightly tied below their trouser knees to guard against escaping rats and mice, and dogs stood by as the stacks grew lower. The loose straw was baled by a "stationary" baler in our day, but before then would have had to be retied by hand as thatching straw was. All straw for stock bedding was restacked. All corn was bagged.

At other seasons between milking and dairy work times, and once the cow sheds were cleaned, I would help old Walter with his two cart horses, and with mud-caked boots would roll or harrow the fields once Walter had ploughed and sown them. My special charge though was Trixie the cobby pony, and we'd cart meal to the poultry or pigs, or I'd even take her or one of the shires to the blacksmith.

These two farms were the last in the district to use horses and scorn milking machines. Combine harvesters were still unknown in our area.'

HARVEST AND THRESHING

'In harvest time at Redbourn in the 1910s we would help by collecting the corn sheaves thrown out by the binder and "throwing them in" ie putting them in clumps of eight or ten sheaves, ready for the men to set up the stooks. This was quite heavy work and there were often thistles in the corn. Mother used to bring a picnic down to the fields in those days. When the corn had dried out, the carting began. We children would help by driving the empty carts to the fields and leading the horses back with full carts to the stackyard where the men were building the ricks.

The ricks when finished would be thatched with straw and left until the threshing tackle came in the spring. This was a noisy and exciting time but too dangerous a job for children to be allowed very near. However, we would dodge under the driving belt and see the corn pouring out into sacks which were loaded onto carts and driven to a barn to be stored until the grain was sold. It was weighed on large scales with a platform on which the sacks were tipped.'

'There were four working farms in Burnham Green in the 1920s. In the summer we used to spend most of our time down the fields watching the corn being harvested. The corn would be cut, pitched out of the machine in a sheath and then about five sheaths were stood on end, these were called "stooks" and left in the field to dry. The great big threshing machine would come and the farm labourers would pitch the corn into this machine with their pitchforks, separating the hay from the grain which was fed into a sack on the machine. When the corn was being cut, rabbits and hares would run from the field, the farmers would shoot them and often the farmer gave us one to take home. Mum would be delighted and rabbit stew was enjoyed by all. We all went gleaning to get corn to feed the chickens and the straw was used for the nests.

The men of the village all had large allotments, as most families were large. The allotments were always referred to as the "Garden Field" and really came into their own during the "Dig for Victory" campaign in the Second World War.

There was also a sausage skin factory in the village and if the wind was blowing in the direction of your house, all doors and windows were shut. The stench was indescribable.'

'A great event of the farm year was the winter threshing when all the neat stacks put up in harvest were threshed

Steam engines and horse-power working together to complete the threshing during the Second World War. (Photograph courtesy of Hitchin Museum)

out with a steam engine (coal at 15 shillings a ton) driving the drum. When the farming stacks were done, my father had a day threshing the gleanings – these were the ears of corn left by the binders and rakes in harvest time and could be collected by young and old between the hours marked by the tolling of the "Gleaners Bell" in the church at Ashwell. For the winter threshing these gleanings arrived in sacks, bags and wheelbarrows to be turned into grain – and woe betide the farmer who muddled Mrs A's with Mrs B's! Today a single combine performs the whole operation of three binders, six to nine horses and the threshing tackle.'

THE BUTCHER, THE BAKER . . .

There was always a job for those who could provide the necessities of life such as bread and meat. With customers relying on them, there was no excuse for not delivering the orders – even when the roads were blocked by deep snow. With every house burning a fire or range to provide warmth and hot water and food, another essential service was that of the chimney sweep, and his 'climbing boy'.

THE ORDER MUST GET THROUGH

'My father worked for two different butchers until after the end of the First World War when he decided to set up on his own. At that time Shenley had three resident butchers and two who visited the village each week, so as you can imagine, competition was fierce and it was very necessary to keep your customers happy. I remember delivering meat to Green Street and have the customer say something like, "Oh! I meant to order some chops for lunch today. Do you think you could bring some back for me?" Then I would have to finish my round, rush back to the shop for the chops and then dash to Green Street so that the customer could have them in time for lunch.

We always tried to get our week-end orders by Thursday so that if we were short of any meat my father could cycle over to Watford on the Friday to pick up what was needed. He would do this however small the extra amount required.

It was one such Friday that I was involved with another person in the shop in making sausages. It took two people to use the machine – one had to feed the meat into the hopper whilst the other turned the handle which revolved the cutting blades. I was pushing the meat into the machine when I let out a yell! One of my fingers had caught in the blades and although my partner stopped turning immediately, it was not soon enough to prevent the end of my finger being almost chopped off. I was rushed to the doctor who managed to patch up my hand. In those days such an injury was not enough to allow you to be off work though I did have to have some time off each day to have my finger dressed. When my father returned from Watford and found out what had happened, he said, "How many times do I have to tell you? Don't push with your fingers – use your knuckles!"

I rode one of those heavy trade cycles which had a carrier in front to take the large wicker basket containing the supplies. In those days, of course, there were no freezers and so locally we made deliveries every day, further afield we visited our customers twice a week, on Wednesdays and Saturdays.

The winter of 1927 was very bad and I remember one day in particular when I had to go out delivering. The road was completely blocked from St Botolph's to the crossroads by Bell Lane with snow piled as high as the hedges either side and was impassable. Obviously I was not going to be able to use the bicycle, so I slung the basket over my arm, filled with the orders to be delivered, and trudged off to try to find a way towards Harper Lane. I went across the land where the hospital now stands, making for Porters Mansion, and then headed towards the golf course. Here there was an iron fence that stretched across the fields in the direction I was heading, and I had to walk on top of this because of the depth of snow on either side. Somehow I managed to get through to three cottages which housed farm workers. They were very surprised to see me even though they knew that my father's philosophy was that customers should not be let down. However, the snow did prevent me from getting down to the shepherd's cottage by the lane. I made my way back across the fields to where the square of Shenleybury houses now stands and so back to the shop. It had been a very difficult trip taking much longer than usual and my father emphasised this fact by his words of greeting – "Where on earth have you been?"'

THE BAKERY

'In 1930 I started work in a large bakery. The only girl on the premises and at that time the only female working in a local bakery. For three months I worked in the tin room greasing, lining and preparing tins of all kinds for seven shillings and sixpence a week, while the management were deciding to let me stay. What a life but stay I did until 1942 and was made very welcome although I was still the only girl in the actual bakery for quite a time. For five years I walked the four miles to work winter and summer at six o'clock in the morning to be at work at 7.15, until we had an early morning bus service.'

'My husband was apprenticed to George Myall, the baker at Letchworth, in 1936. The small bakehouse was situated next to the Triangle Stores at the point of Glebe Road running into Common View. About 1937/38 Mr Myall had an up to date bakehouse built in Icknield Way next to the Marmet pram factory – with a lovely house in front for his family to live in, on the premises so to speak. He ran a competition in the local paper to find a new name for his bakery. I don't remember who won but the name "The Letchworth Bakery" was chosen. By this time my husband, growing up fast, was well on the way to being "the right hand man" and training for master confectioner. On Good Friday, hot cross bun day, it was usual to report for work at 6am on the Thursday and work through till the delivery of buns from 4–5am Friday. They were thrown up to the customer at their bedroom window (six to a bag) really hot and new. Couldn't happen these days!

Sadly Mr Myall lost my husband to the army in 1942, and by the time he had finished his war service in 1945, Mr Myall had died and the business had been sold. The bakehouse is no more but the family home remains in Icknield Way.'

THE SWEEP

'Within living memory there was a "climbing boy" at Aldbury – Edwin Garment, whose father pushed him up the chimneys and gained a precarious livelihood by selling the soot brought down to the farmers to put on their fields. Little Edwin climbed up the chimney with a hood over his head and a scraper in one hand and the brush in the other – there was no cruelty involved such as that referred to in *Oliver Twist*. The sweep had a little donkey which grazed on any of the three open fields when "the crops be rid".'

'Tommy Barcock the sweep at Baldock between the wars drove a pony and trap and had a mongrel dog to guard the bags of soot. He always called little girls who were sent on errands by their mums to make a booking, "My dear". He was always late for his appointments and was considered to be the dirtiest sweep in the area. To us girls, the most fascinating thing about him was the lack of one hand which had been replaced by a wicked iron hook.'

ON THE ESTATE

Landed estates and the 'big house' offered employment to many in Hertfordshire, with a variety of trades and occupations from gardeners to housemaids.

THE GARDENER

'I married in 1927 and my husband became the Head Gardener at the estate of Mr Henry Loyd at Langleybury, Hunton Bridge, Kings Langley. There were many greenhouses in which were grown vines, peaches, melons and carnations, all of which were served by two huge boilers which had to be stoked regularly to keep up the temperature. All the flowers which were grown were taken to the Mansion House before breakfast each day and had to be arranged within the house. My husband also had to arrange all the flowers when there were flower shows and garden parties.

Many big shoots were held and the men and boys came to beat the birds out of the bushes. The butler, footmen and hallboy were taken to "Temple Pan", the shooting lodge, in a shooting brake so they could lay out all the food for lunch.'

THE MAID

I was 16 years old when I went to work for Lord and Lady Desborough at Panshanger, Hertingfordbury, and the year was 1925. I started work as a laundry maid (goffering all pillowcase and nightdress frills) whilst waiting to become a stillroom maid. Panshanger was Lady Desborough's favourite home and we were in residence twice a year, at Easter and in October, most of their entertaining being done here as the house was larger than Lord Desborough's favourite home, Taplow Court near Maidenhead.

There were 17 members of indoor staff at Panshanger. We stillroom maids wore a blue dress with white apron, plain white cap, black stockings and black shoes in the mornings, then in the afternoons a black dress with white apron and frilly cap. Our duties included the early morning tea and breakfast trays, making jams, preserves and marmalades, bottling and making breakfast rolls. The main job was afternoon tea, for which we would make scones and about 14 kinds of little cakes as well as large ones. Twice a day a cowman would bring in milk from the Jersey herd, and we had to take some to the dairy and make butter.

When the family were entertaining, Lady Desborough always enjoyed making up bath salts to suit her guests; we would prepare the Steward's room for her and lay out the salts, colourings and perfumes in readiness.

Lord Desborough would not have any of his clocks altered for British Summer Time, so there were two sets of clocks – one showing His Lordship's time and the other showing the outside world's time.

Lady Desborough always celebrated St Thomas' Day, when all the indoor staff and the ground staff would meet and be served warm ale with bread and cheese, prepared by the stillroom. I think this was a custom passed down by Lord Cowper.

Lord Desborough always called us "his girls" – they were a wonderful family to work for and we were a very happy staff; we saw the best of society, we learnt manners and speech, and how to behave generally. It was like one big family, a lovely life, and I don't regret it one bit.'

PART OF VILLAGE LIFE

'Before the First World War the estates of the gentry provided much employment for village girls and boys at Little Munden both indoors and in gardens and stables. Cooks, scullery maids, housekeepers, butlers, footmen, grooms, not forgetting the 'Lamps and Boots'. The latter was a full time job to fill and trim oil lamps for each room and corridor in the mansion. Farmers too relied on the men as ploughmen, cowmen, shepherds, thatchers, hedgers and for general farm work for all seasons. Hours were long and work hard but men gave their all to the welfare of their animals. Cattle and sheep were driven to market by drovers starting early and walking in my area up to 15 miles. Men often walked some distance to work using the footpaths which sadly now have disappeared.

The wheelwright and farrier of the village too were kept busy with work from the farms: new shoes for horses, rims for carts and waggons, sharpening of ploughshares and resetting of harrows. The County Council even in the early days employed men to cover "stretches" as they were called, of the road verges and banks. Each man had a section to keep clear of weeds, clean out gulleys, cut the grass banks and hedges. They were proud of their stretch.'

GETTING ABOUT

For most people during the first decades of the century, 'getting about' meant walking – or going by pony and trap if you were lucky. Cars were still a rarity until after the Second World War, and the quirks of the first cars are remembered with affection. For work, for school or for play, people cycled, went by bus or caught the local train – but that, of course, was before the Beeching cuts axed so many little local railway stations.

LIFE WITHOUT A CAR

'We walked in our village – no cars, no fumes and no danger to children. But we had to walk a long way. Once a week the Baker family opened all the gates of Bayford-bury and the surrounding land. This meant a short cut to Hertford, so a steady stream of villagers left to walk to Hertford, usually on Saturday to the big market. Horse and cart was another means of transport used by trades-men, farmers and for any jobs about the village, eg removals. Young people were later to own bicycles and they biked everywhere. Steam trains by LNER were for a real treat, up the line to London. When buses eventually ran from Bayford to Hertford, everyone crammed on them and frequently you had to stand all the way.'

'You walked everywhere in the 1930s and 1940s. I didn't get a bike till I was in my early teens. On market days in Hemel market square, we'd walk from Potten End, com-ing along all the old lanes that aren't there any more.'

'Early in the 1950s we went to my cousin's christening. It took place in a church about five miles from where my aunt and uncle lived. They were, at that time, living with my aunt's parents and her six brothers and sisters. It must have been very cramped, even in a four-bedroomed council house.

After the ceremony Mum, baby and two grandmas drove off in the only car with my uncle. The rest of us waited half an hour for a bus. There were 20 of us and the conductor wound off about ten ft of ticket on his machine. Luckily it was a dry sunny day, as even when the bus reached our stop we still had another ten minutes walk to the house, and by then we were ready for a very welcome cup of tea.'

The demand for bicycles between the wars meant business was good for this cycle maker from Hemel Hempstead.

169

THE FIRST CARS

'I remember our first car – a De Dion, which went about five or six miles if you were lucky, before getting a puncture when the stepney wheel had to be fitted. To actually get from A to B it was a dogcart for my father and the "tub" (a square cart) for my mother, with a nice quiet pony. She would take elderly friends and relatives for "a little drive" around Ashwell.'

'My mother, who was born in 1896, was brought up at the Mill House on the river in Standon, where her father was the flour miller. She used to enthral me with tales of childhood trips to Puckeridge with the family in the pony and trap and of the icy day when the pony slipped and fell on a hill, turning the trap over and tipping them all into the ditch.

Later, before the First World War, her father bought a motor car and when she was 17, he taught my mother to drive. His precept for safe driving was to "keep on the crown of the road". When she drove through the lanes children shouted, "There's a lady driving" and took to the hedges in trepidation.

At 19 my mother took an RAC public service vehicle driving test, coached by a taxi driver, to become a voluntary ambulance driver in the war. During the test the taxi's engine stalled and the driver, who was sitting in the back, had to jump out to crank the engine into life with its starting handle. I still have the little cardboard driving licence with her photograph in it, dated 14th May 1915, certifying that my mother was qualified to drive a taxi-cab!'

'One of my aunts was the proud possessor of a car and my cousin and I used to sit in the dickey seat behind, proud as anything.'

'Watford could boast that it had one of the first AA boxes in the country and it was manned by a Mr Drew, who was the first AA patrolman to be appointed.'

'In the 1950s we either walked or cycled everywhere. Only a few people owned cars, and one who did was our next door neighbour who was the proud possessor of a green and black Austin Seven. One never to be forgotten day in high summer I was taken in their car to Snettisham on the Norfolk coast to go cockling. What fun it was, a rare day spent by the sea, accompanied by a large picnic basket packed full of good things, including soggy tomato sandwiches and large slabs of home-made fruit cake.'

ON THE BUSES

'Transport was usually by bus. Trips to St Albans from Watford in the 1920s were by open topped double decker buses along St Albans Road, along country lanes almost to St Albans itself. A workman's ticket of one shilling would take you from Watford Junction to London, providing you arrived at the station by 7am. This was also a return fare. The other method of travel was the first Green Line coaches, most of the journey being through country lanes. Hard to believe these days.

The cheapest way of getting around was to walk. Down through Cassiobury Park, over the golf links and into Whippindell Woods. Or up the Harebreaks on to Leavesden as far as the Hare pub, through a footpath across the fields out on to the Orbital road and so back home. These were just a couple of Sunday afternoon strolls when my husband was my boyfriend.'

'When I visited my grandparents at Shenley as a child before the 1940s, it meant travelling by train to Radlett station and walking two miles, or coming via Golders

171

Buses were a reliable and friendly way to travel, an alternative to bicycling or Shanks's pony!

Green and getting an open-topped bus to Ridge Hill and walking the two miles up the lanes. When the buses came to Shenley they were very friendly. There were no proper stops, if you wanted the bus you just put out your hand! My aunt was a daily passenger to Borehamwood and as the bus started at the pond, if she was not aboard at the time of departure, the conductor would walk up to her house and say they were ready to go!'

GOING BY TRAIN

'My father had a clock erected on the top of the stables on the other side of the lane from our house at Park Street. Irate late risers would call to us as they ran for the train, "Tell your father the clock's wrong again." In the dry days of summer, sparks from the engine used to set the railway bank alight as it puffed up the lane and with one accord

172

we four children would seize sacks that had been soaked in water, climb the fence and act as firefighters, to return filthy to the house when the fire was put out.'

'There was a local railway that ran from Welwyn Garden City to Luton via Ayot Green. Luton, centre of the hat industry, gave many village ladies the chance to earn some money in the factories. Sadly, the station burned down in 1948 and was never replaced and the line was closed in 1965.'

'I remember watching as the viaduct that runs through the valley at Digswell had its red bricks taken out and replaced with blue ones in 1930. That was a sight to see.'

'I travelled to school at Bishops Stortford in the late 1950s by train. I was able to travel to the station with my father but from then on was on my own. He went in to London, I went in the opposite direction. The Victorian station was small and still quite rural in character with well tended flower beds, and porters who called out, "Broxbourne, this is Broxbourne, Roydon, Harlow, Burnt Mill, Sawbridgeworth, Bishops Stortford train. Change here for . . ." I can still hear it in my mind. It was quite characteristic and we soon became proficient at it ourselves.

The trains were cosy. Pulled by small steam engines with a homely chug, the trains had separate compartments and we used to vie for the window seat. I guess they were old rolling stock, with faded brown seat covers and a feeling of faded opulence. We had new luggage racks and framed pictures on the walls of far-away beauty spots like Hutton-le-Hole.

Along the route there were particular places of note. At Rye House we passed the new power station and were subject to a particular chemical smell which to this day I associate with Bell & Websters. At Roydon we watched fishermen. Burnt Mill station, later to become Harlow's main station, was the prettiest of all the stations, with a profusion of flowers all year, or so it seemed.

Just outside Sawbridgeworth station was an elongated hillock. We always called it the Long Barrow, but I don't know whether any archaeological work was ever done there to substantiate this claim. The approach to Bishops Stortford station was marked by the maltings and the smell of warm barley that was always around the town. Having survived the train ride it was now time to heave on the leather window strap, open the window and alight from the train. It was while travelling to school that I learned how to jump smartly from the train before it quite stopped. I never did master the reverse, getting aboard after the train had started! The journey was completed by joining the stream of girls walking up Warwick Road to the school.

At this time there were First and Third class carriages and we had to be careful to get in the right one. This was far more critical on the rare and exciting occasions when we had a corridor train and the inspector travelled with us. The trains were pretty reliable although frozen points could cause delays in winter and once in a while our train would be cancelled and it was a great thrill to travel on the main-line Cambridge train via Bishops Stortford which was especially stopped at Broxbourne to pick us up. Oh the folly of living near Broxbourne, the others got the day off!

Most of these things were to change, First and Third class became First and Second; the locomotives changed from steam to diesel, and before I left the line was electrified and the stations not only rebuilt, but in some cases renamed.'

WAR & PEACE

THE GREAT WAR

Though the First World War was fought away from England's shores, the people of Hertfordshire had their first taste of aerial warfare as the cigar-shaped Zeppelins were seen in the skies. Prisoners of war worked on local farms, and soldiers became a common sight on the county's roads. The civilian population faced hardship and shortages through the long years, and the celebrations that greeted the ending of the war were heartfelt indeed.

SOLDIERS, PRISONERS AND ZEPPELINS

'I was born in a farmhouse in Ashwell in which my forebears had lived for several hundred years. We have all been farmers and have seen many changes over the years, starting in my memory with the 1914–18 war when all the men who were fit were called up, their places later being taken by German prisoners of war, of whom we had five. They made a great fuss of me as a child and I loved them!

My father's hunters were commandeered by the Army and there was an air of great sadness as he rode his favourite "Spider" out of the farm gates for the last time to take her to Biggleswade, which was our area's collecting centre. All the farm men stood in a line to see them go.

Another vivid memory I have is of being taken by my mother down to Ashwell Hospital. Mr and Mrs Wolverley Fordham had generously handed over Ashwell Bury as a convalescent home for wounded soldiers. The cleaning, cooking and nursing were carried out almost exclusively by Ashwell people who also provided many of the provisions, ie flour, sausages, vegetables, eggs, groceries – not

Horsepower was still essential for the soldier of the First World War and sights such as this at Handpost Farm, Hemel Hempstead were common in the country.

to mention daily papers, entrance to cinemas, haircuts and an endless supply of nightshirts and blue knitted socks made by village working parties.

Mrs Fordham was Commandant, my aunt the Quartermaster. "Dear old Quarter – if you don't get a medal you oughter" wrote one of the soldiers in a book she kept for their comments.'

'My father joined the army during the First World War. Soldiers were sent to guard the viaduct as Digswell, as it was an important link to the north.'

'During the war soldiers from the Westminster Rifles were billeted in Leverstock Green and used to exercise their horses on the Green. One lady's mother made meat pies and sold them to the families visiting the soldiers.'

177

'I remember hearing my mother talk of the Boer War, because my father fought in it and I have his medal. I also remember the start of the First World War, the war that was to end all wars. Most of us know what happened about that. Soldiers were billeted in Bovingdon and the gun carriages would pass our cottage every morning.'

'We had a German prisoner of war camp, opposite where our railway station at Welham Green is today. My father was a builder in the village and he had to build a brick silo for Mr Crawford at Potterells Farm and he had two Germans from the camp helping him; they learned quite a lot of English and it was great fun listening to them.'

'Rations during the war were meagre and mothers became resourceful in using aids to add to the larder: marrow jam, adding cornflour to margarine, and creaming the milk of its cream and shaking this in a jam jar to make butter – a lot of shaking for a little butter. We kept chickens and reared two pigs annually, feeding them on the boiled potato peelings and scrapings from the porridge saucepan and dishes. These were slaughtered, one every six months. As children we hated the day "Bimmer" was killed and scalded in the boiling water. The pig killer walked three miles to Little Munden and it took him all day – payment seven shillings and sixpence. Mother retained the offal, head and trotters which she made into brawn, faggots and chitterlings from the intestines, the latter taking hours to wash and turn in salt water. Many neighbours shared these goodies but, with no deep freezers, they had to be consumed over a few days.'

'I remember walking to Hertford with mother and queuing in Maidenhead Street outside the Home & Colonial to get half a pound of margarine (which was horrible) and one egg. This was before we were rationed. I also remember watching the Zeppelins going over to bomb London. They looked like large cigars.'

'I lived in the end one of three cottages (now gone) near the top of Station Road in Broxbourne, which was then a country lane with just Pulham's stonemason's premises and the Welcome Cafe on the way to the pub near the station. During the war I remember being held up by my father to see a silver cigar-shaped Zeppelin drift over. "You'll never see a sight like that again as long as you live," he said. At school air raid practice consisted of diving under the big desks.'

'The central point of Essendon village is still its church. On 3rd September 1916 a bomb from a Zeppelin dropped, doing terrible damage to the church and killing two young Bamford sisters in a cottage nearby.'

'I was very little at the time of the war, but Auntie Nellie, who lived next door to us at Southdown, Harpenden used to take care of me if an air raid warning sounded, until the all clear went. There was only one incident, when a Zeppelin was brought down at Cuffley. After the war there was a large gun remaining on the Common where the soldiers drilled.

After the war was over, races were held on the Common for all schools in the neighbourhood. There were Peace Day celebrations in Clarence Park in St Albans and each child was given a beaker with a picture of the world and doves of peace.'

'I was ten years old when the first war started and the needlework mistress at my school was also the local Red Cross Commandant (voluntary in those days, I think). This wonderful lady made sure we were all "useful". We knitted socks, mittens and balaclavas for soldiers and on

Saturday mornings, some of us did "gardening" – as far as I remember it was washing pots etc in the grounds of one of the many lovely houses at the top of Stamford Hill, which had become an Auxiliary Military Hospital. I suppose nowadays, someone would say it was exploiting children, but it was no such thing. We all enjoyed ourselves, we were kept out of mischief and we were taught to be "useful citizens".

I was 14 when the Armistice was signed and during the four years of war I had lost uncles and several cousins in the Army and RFC. One close cousin had run away from school at 17 to join the RFC, went right through the war and was blown up in Belgium after the Armistice – he was just 21. I remember the air raids on London and I saw two Zepps come down – the first at Cuffley and the second at Potters Bar. I wonder how many people these days stop to look at the memorial to Capt Robinson erected at the top of Plough Hill, Cuffley? The inscription tells how this wonderful young man brought down the first "Zeppy" on British soil "After having been in the air for more than two hours." In these days of comfortable flying, this caption seems ludicrous, but when you think, those boys flew in unheated open cockpits and wore no special clothing of pure silk, cashmere etc as in the later war; they must have been nearly frozen.'

THE SECOND WORLD WAR

Just over 20 years later, the people of Hertfordshire were at war again. This time the civilian population was a part of the conflict and air raids became a 'normal' part of life, particularly for children growing up in those years.

GROWING UP IN WARTIME

'I well remember the day war was declared and the sombre look on my parents' faces, but not understanding the reason for it. My dad, fortunately, was a little too old to be called up, so he served as an Air Raid Precaution Officer and patrolled round the village of Waterford each night to make sure there were no cracks of light in people's curtains. A few children were evacuated to the village, but we just looked after our relatives who would escape from the London bombing and come and stay with us for periods of time – we sometimes had as many as 20 people sleeping on the floors (under the kitchen table was our air raid shelter!) Two of my cousins actually lived with us for quite a long time and went to the local secondary school. On one occasion, as a German plane was leaving London, it showered the village with incendiary bombs but fortunately they fell in the fields rather than on the houses.'

'I still have my ration book cover which I made at school. Being only very small I remember odd things, such as the planes at Breachwood Green, fighter planes shooting at the enemy, and big tanks rolling past our house. A barricade was put across the road to stop the enemy and I had to climb over it to get to school. At school, we wrote in a tray of sand as there was a paper shortage, and we were joined by London evacuees.'

'About 1941–42 my parents had an official visit from officers at the REME camp at Cupid Green (now Grove Hill). They asked how many bedrooms we had and how many children were in our house, and we were told we would have a number of soldiers billeted on us. They were only to sleep, no food was to be given. My mother was paid sixpence a night. One young soldier of 17 years came to us from Swindon and to this day is a valued friend.'

'The war started when I was eleven. It was a trying time for my parents as we had a three bedroomed house and it was decided by the government that we had plenty of room for lodgers. We children had to sleep in the sitting room where the Morrison shelter was. We first had two nurses who were to work at the base hospital, opposite Leavesden mental hospital, opened especially for the casualties expected. The nurses stayed for several months. After them we had two men billeted on us, and they were to work at Leavesden aerodrome.

I didn't enjoy school much, but I remember a competition run by Cadbury's. They wanted an essay about chocolate. I wrote about Africa and the cocoa bean, and I won first prize which consisted of several bars of chocolate. In war torn Britain and sweet rationing, it was quite something to win! I was surprised and delighted.'

'I remember the old elm tree at Aldbury, always known as "Bunyan's Tree" because he was supposed to have preached under it. During the war it had a sentry box round it, known as a "flower pot". Later it had to be felled because of disease.'

'In September 1939 when war broke out, I was in the sixth form at school and we only went in once a week to collect work and give in homework while the air raid trenches were dug. We larked about while sticking brown paper tape on the school windows, but it was a bit scary later on, taking our turns sleeping on the floor on fire bomb duty. I had five miles to go on a train and after an air raid the worst thing was wondering as you went home, whether your house would still be there.

In 1942, I went to a horticultural college and we spent a lot of time digging a ten pole allotment for marks towards the exam and vegetables for the kitchen. We got especially hungry working out of doors and on the way home used to buy filling malt loaves which were not rationed then. We did air raid warden duties and helped at the local hospital – mostly washing up, and I had fun helping to run a Brownie pack.

When I was at work in Kent as a Field Officer on hop disease experiments, we were among the barrage balloons and sometimes had to dive into ditches when the doodle-bugs came over. I have vivid memories of the heart-stopping moment of sudden silence as the engine cut out and we waited for the explosion.

We had a keen group of bell ringers who practised on muffled bells, waiting for the day when peace would be declared and the victory peals could ring out. I rang in a quarter peal and had blisters on my hands to prove it! Sometimes we went "Tower-snatching" when we would ring changes in three or four different villages. The comradeship of the ringers was typical of the war-time spirit that kept England going through the dark days.'

'Along the A41 between Berkhamsted and Northchurch were prefabricated buildings housing German prisoners of war. A few were allowed to attend St Mary's church, Northchurch. They wore dark brown battledress-type uniform and I remember feeling so sad for them sitting quietly in the church. My friend and I (about twelve years old) were quite in love with the best looking one, because as he walked back to the camp he had winked at us!'

AIR RAIDS

'Although we were so close to Potters Bar at Little Heath, we were not allowed air raid shelters, though unlike the authorities, the bombers couldn't see the boundary stone and we did get a few dropped in the area. We could see lots of barrage balloons from our house flying over London, and the occasional dog fight in the air.

We had an evacuee from Highgate – no room to put him but that didn't matter. When my mother was taken to hospital I had to look after the house and him. I remember having to give him Parrishes Food which he sucked through a straw so that his teeth did not get stained.

Later on I got a job as a chemist's assistant. One day a land mine was dropped a few streets away and all the shelves shook and the hundreds of bottles were smashed. What a mess! That was too close for comfort.

Cosmetics were in very short supply, so my boss decided to manufacture a range of his own. These proved to be quite popular. I was his guinea pig for "liquid stockings". What a mess that made of everything – clothes and bed linen especially.'

'I was born in 1915 and lived on the borders of Hertfordshire and Middlesex. I grew up with hatred of the Germans instilled in me. My father worked at the Royal Small Arms factory in Enfield Lock and this was a target in both wars, especially during the Second World War, and many bombs were dropped around the area. A V2 rocket bomb dropped and completely destroyed the junior school which I had attended and did much damage around. Our

184

house had windows blown in and ceilings down.

My husband was called up into the army in 1940 and we married shortly afterwards as he was drafted overseas after only three months. He was sent to Malta where he endured four most dreadful years of intense bombing and destruction. At home we slept in dugouts in the garden at night; made of corrugated iron and buried in the ground, they were called Anderson shelters after the man who invented them. Sometimes we would wake up to find water seeping through the sides and had to bale out. Later we braved it indoors and slept under the dining room table or in the cupboard under the stairs. I can remember seeing the reflections in the sky of the huge fires burning in London after the bombing by the Germans. I also remember seeing aerial dog fights of German and English planes over the Thames estuary. This was from the Cheshunt club where we played tennis in between bombing raids. Some Italian prisoners of war were sent to Cheshunt to work on the land and in the nurseries, and many of the men stayed on after the war.

Food was severely rationed with one egg per week, or even one egg in two weeks, but we coped; we had all laid in stocks of sugar, flour etc beforehand and eked this out. With clothes we had to make do with our allotted coupons but we didn't need many stylish or smart clothes, there was nowhere to go. Of an evening we just stayed in and listened to the radio. At the end of the war when my husband came home we went in for our first baby straight away. There was a celebration street party where I lived and I can remember sitting there in the road at a long table with my baby in my lap, having such fun singing and shouting the war is over!'

'During the late 1930s and early 1940s I attended the British school in College Road, Cheshunt. All children had to take a tin to school (mine was a large Oxo tin) and we had to put chocolate items in this tin as emergency rations in the event of an air raid. Many of the children had a telling off from Miss Day, the headmistress, because we had eaten our goodies. In my tin very often the Maltesers had been eaten and only the paper wrappers remained.'

'I was born in 1942 in a little house called "Firtree" opposite the church of Essendon. I can still recall having to lie under the large farmhouse kitchen table every time the sirens went off, and all I could see from there was the black kitchen range. Our village school was damaged by a flying bomb (a "doodlebug") one Saturday morning in 1945. My two brothers and sisters went there, as did my parents and their families earlier. The gap in our village would have been great if the bomb had dropped on a schoolday. Because of the damage, children could no longer use the school, so the local village hall was made into a school. I was also very lucky that day as the bomb brought my bedroom ceiling down on my cot.'

'When the Second World War came, the stables at Langleybury were made into "shelters" as Equity & Law from Lincoln's Inn rented the mansion. The field in front of our house had guns and searchlights in it. The soldiers were under canvas and had water from the bothy until mains water was laid on, and came to our house for baths. When the ATS arrived, huts were put up and the girls soon had them shipshape with flowers. Many years after, one of the girls came back to thank my husband for making her wedding bouquet.

I also helped at Model Farm when the threshing machine came and with my children, we put up the shocks of corn. We also picked up potatoes in the fields with the horse and cart following behind to pick up the sacks. As our house was used as a post, we could only bathe between 6 and 6.30pm because the bath was upstairs and at night the top floor was taken over by the ARP. The signal for enemy aircraft coming over was given as "orange", and "purple" meant that they had gone elsewhere. One night 16 bombs fell across the meadows.'

'Being a teenager during the war meant many changes; sharing our home with evacuees, making sure the black-out blinds didn't show any chinks of light outside which would have meant a knock on the door by the local ARP warden, sleeping on a make-shift bed under the dining table when the blitz was at its worst and sharing my mother's anxiety over Dad who, being in the National Fire Service, was being sent all over the south of England fighting fires.

I remember volunteering to help the local ARP. They needed two "gas victims" to practise on should a real gas attack ever happen. We were asked to put on our bathing costumes under our clothes and report to the local depot. My friend and I were startled to find ourselves transported to the mortuary at the Watford Peace Memorial Hospital where we were stripped to our costumes and hosed down with very cold water. We were very careful what we volunteered for after that episode. Another memory of an incident of that particular hospital was when I was with the Guides and we were working for our proficiency badges. A friend and I were helping in the kitchens using a machine that made breadcrumbs. To my horror my Guide badge was missing from my tie and to this day, I think it must have dropped into the bread-crumbs. What nightmares I had about the awful consequences that could have occurred.

A frightening incident which sticks in my mind was at the time of the V1 bombs (doodlebugs as they were called). My mother and I heard the noise of one approaching our home and then there was that awful silence when the engine stopped which indicated it was about to fall. There was a loud rush of air as the object passed over our house and a terrifying explosion as it hit houses two roads away, luckily without loss of life.'

'During the war, my husband and I lived at Eleanor Cross Road, Waltham Cross, my husband being a member of a firewatching team whose meeting point was the Conservative Club. The siren went in the early hours of one morning and after waking him, he got out of bed, put his socks on and promptly got back in again. After much poking and prodding he dressed and went off. One of his colleagues was the local dentist and another the barman at the club. The barman had forgotten the key, the dentist had to go back for his teeth and the other member of the team didn't come at all. The barman went home, collected the key and opened up. It was a very cold night and somebody suggested a whisky would help to keep the cold out. They decided the bar was the best place to firewatch. My husband returned home four hours later slightly inebriated, two hours after the all clear had gone, having not heard it although the siren was outside the Conservative Club.'

BOMBED OUT

'My first memories of Hertfordshire are of the autumn of 1941 when I was nine years old; the countryside, the small village school, and milk purchased at the farm from a large churn, and many other things so different from my life in London.

On 18th September 1940 at about 11.30pm, as was the usual practice my family did not go to bed, but went straight into our Anderson air raid shelter. This was in our back garden, where a large hole had been dug in the ground and a shelter built around the corrugated iron. My father had made it very cosy inside, matting on the floor, bunkbeds and a few other home comforts.

There was my mother, father and brother who was three years younger than me. We also had a soldier billeted with us. A Sergeant Major training cadets at the local polytechnic, he was married with children. It was the first time he had been stationed without his family with him; they were at home in Birmingham. His children had been born in India and Egypt, so had always in the past travelled with the army. We called him Uncle Harry.

At about 11.30pm my mother heard a flapping noise outside the shelter and thought it was a German airman who had baled out of a plane, as there had been bombing and heavy gunfire from early evening. My father and Uncle Harry opened the shelter door to see what it was and then the bomb went off. We knew afterwards it was a land-mine; they came down on parachutes. The back of our shelter was blown out and my brother and I were covered in earth. My mother was crying, Uncle Harry was killed and my father was pulling our two lady neighbours from their shelter as it sank into a large crater caused by the explosion and a burst water main. I remember looking towards our house and it was just a pile of rubble with smoke rising from it. We had to be taken out of our shelter as quickly as possible. My father was blowing his ARP whistle and when help came we were carried to public air raid shelters and had to stay there until the morning when the all clear sounded.

We then had to stay with my grandparents, as we had no home and no clothes, only our pyjamas and siren suit which we were wearing at the time, but people helped each other any way they could.

My father worked for a company that owned a large country house in Hertfordshire which they used for entertaining and business functions. It had tennis courts, a bowling green and extensive gardens. It was called Shendish House; from the main road the drive was about a mile long, it was a beautiful place. The company decided to let the rooms off into flats for employees and their families who had been made homeless by the blitz. They also provided furnishings etc and all that we required, my father was to pay them back over a period of time. They were so good, we were the first family to arrive there, but in due course a few other families joined us. This was in October 1940 and in April 1941, I had a new baby sister, my mother called her Shenda.'

THE EVACUEES

The exodus of children from the crowded streets of London began immediately. Though many were sent further afield, it was not long before Hertfordshire received its first influx of bewildered refugees.

TAKING THE CHILDREN IN

'The effects of the war were not too bad in Bayford, with farms all around and the villagers mostly self-sufficient in vegetables and fruit. Farmers and farm workers received an extra ration of cheese and an egg because of their job.

When the billeting man came round most people were forced to take one or two evacuees. These children had never been to the country. They arrived from the cities in a very poor condition, with skin diseases, impetigo and dirty heads. Eighty children from Dr Barnardo's came to Bayford, which overcrowded the school and wasn't too popular.

Ashendene House became a hospital where operations were performed; I remember helping to sew the blackout curtains. The Manor House became a convalescent home.

We had a Home Guard in the village, and villagers became wardens and patrolled to ensure the blackout was kept. We used to watch them exercise in Bayford Park. They also did fire-watching and often had to share helmets, passing them from watch to watch.'

'In 1939 I was living in London with my mother, father and two brothers. When the war began my brothers and I were evacuated to St Albans. I thought it was great fun until I saw my mother crying. I think I grew up then. My brothers and I were hard to place as there were three of us and eventually we were separated, but in January 1940, as the war seemed far away, my mother took us back to London. I remember feeling so proud of being British at one point that I walked through Clarence Park singing *There'll always be an England*!'

'September 1st 1939 saw a mass exodus of children from London as evacuees. Although I should have gone with my secondary school, I was evacuated with the junior school I'd recently left at eleven years as my sister aged nine was still there.

We went to a railway station and we were put on a train that ended up in Hertford. No-one seemed to know where we were going, or what would be happening to us so I guess many of the other children felt as I did – poor little "orphans".

First of all we were taken to Hartham and then the group from my junior school with Miss O'Donovan, the first year teacher, were taken to the Drill Hall in Bengeo where we met our hosts. My sister and I shared a billet in Duncombe Road with an unmarried brother and sister who were kindness itself.

Evacuees arriving at Hitchin station in 1943, gas masks carried in their boxes over one shoulder. (Photograph courtesy of Hitchin Museum)

September 1st was a Friday, and on Sunday 3rd my sister and I must have gone to morning Sunday school as we came "home" to find my mother and grandparents had come to see us and tell us that at 11am that morning war had been declared on Germany.

Everything was very strange for us children brought up in North London – we were used to the well tended parks near our home, but the countryside with open fields and rough stony paths was something new and exciting. We went for long walks and saw plants and animals we'd never encountered before. We went blackberrying – not quite so much fun as you got nasty scratches and became entangled with the briars.

On one occasion we saw our first Spitfires flying overhead – on a glorious sunny day in Panshanger Wood. It seems so incongruous looking back!

Later as the war progressed, and we stayed longer than we'd expected, we saw the red glow of fires over London. And towards the end of the war I remember lying in bed one Sunday morning and hearing a doodlebug (V1) fly over and cut out – to learn later that it had fallen into the river bank by Mill Bridge.

Quite early on our hostess sent my sister to her friend's house round the corner, to ask for some thyme. Not knowing what she was asking for my sister asked for some "minutes" please! This found its way into the local press as the friend's husband worked for the Herts Mercury.

For a short time we shared the local village school, but after a while the few older ones among us went to the local grammar school so I found myself at Ware and was in Miss Stoke's form – Upper 3S. At that time Ware Grammar School occupied the site now known as Ware College – opposite the railway crossing.

It was an old rambling building with odd shaped classrooms and twisty corridors, for one end of it had originally been two or three private houses and the school must have encompassed these and the lovely gardens behind as it grew in numbers, until it had to add on some purpose-built classrooms and a hall and gym for the upper school.

One of its beauties was the Gilpin window, telling the story of John Gilpin's mad ride from Edmonton to Ware; on the staircase leading to the house Sixth and Biology rooms. How I loved that window.

Many of the grass tennis courts were turned into a kitchen garden for the duration and provided most of the vegetables used for school dinners. Yet another was despoiled so the school could have an air raid shelter where we would go when the siren sounded – rather dank and joyless, and I don't remember doing much work there. Miss Brettell, our gym mistress, was a past master at Swedish gym and many's the practice we had on summer days out on the one remaining lawn to rousing Sousa marches. I loved netball and finally was in the school team and played in many matches against other schools – usually on a Saturday morning. The most enjoyable ones were the close finishes. The top netball court made a wonderful slide in icy, snowy weather, and many winter playtimes in the junior school were spent happily sliding or playing harmless snowball fights.

I'd been a keen Brownie pre-war and had looked forward to going on to Guides in September 1939, but this was not to be. However in 1943 a new friend joined our form and persuaded several of us that we'd like to be Sea Rangers. She got in touch with the District Commissioner and we were able to reform the SRS (Sea Ranger Ship) Cutty Sark in Hertford. This opened up a whole new life for me which included camping both in Herts and further afield and also led to a lifetime commitment to Guiding.'

'My first realisation that war was a reality was when I was twelve˙ on Friday 1st September, when the evacuees arrived in Stevenage.

They had come by train, this group of frightened and some crying children. They were being shepherded slowly along the road by their teachers and the evacuating officer. The children were clutching cases and brown paper carrier bags which contained all their possessions. Each child wore a label and had their gasmask slung across their back.

The weary group stopped and knocked at each house. The housewife came to the door and came out and selected the child or children according to how many they could fit in, or if they were brothers and sisters. Finally there was a family of five. The girl was the eldest, about nine or ten, with four younger brothers. The people next door to us had the girl with the youngest boy who was about four. The three boys all went to another house. The girl kept the one toothbrush between them all.

Two or three weeks later their father came down in a very large Buick with several drinking friends and took them all home, in spite of the fact they didn't want to go.

We didn't have an evacuee as mother was badly crippled with rheumatoid arthritis and couldn't cope on her own, so my father was not evacuated from London with his office but finally worked in Stevenage and Hertford for a while. In good weather he would cycle the twelve miles there and back.

Owing to mother's disability we were allowed to run a car for her benefit. We had petrol coupons for two or three gallons a month to drive in a five mile area, which meant we could shop in Hitchin or Letchworth. Dad had to keep a log of our trips. We would often give lifts to servicemen especially those going to Henlow where my cousin was stationed. Petrol was three shillings and sixpence a gallon.

At the start of the war, trenches were dug round the hockey pitch at my school in Hitchin for air raid protection, but they appeared to be more of a hazard than a safety protection as fast wingers tended to disappear down them head first in a most unladylike fashion! So they were filled in.

The main corridor by the gymnasium was strengthened with stout timber for safety. If the siren sounded everyone trooped out of the classrooms and into various downstairs corridors and continued with their lessons sitting on benches. To give the Germans credit they usually picked a maths lesson for this exercise.

As the school was on the top of the hill, beside the water tower, troops were stationed on the tower to spot enemy aircraft. Those in adjacent classrooms had their own binoculars to spot the troops! Each term when school started there was a banner draped around the tower saying "Welcome back to school".

Both Hitchin girls and boys schools had scholars from Eastbourne evacuated on them. We went to school in the mornings and they went in the afternoons. Senior pupils were fitted in for more classes. Some Eastbourne pupils stayed on after the war.

Senior girls were allowed a week off in dreary November to go "spud picking" for five shillings a day. Hard work it was too in fog and rain with galvanized buckets weighing a ton, half full of sticky clay with inches of clay on the outside and room for half a dozen potatoes in the middle. The fun of sitting on a wobbly upturned bucket with a sharp bottom in the middle of a dank cold field eating sandwiches, or if you were lucky sitting in the hay in a Dutch barn where they paid seven shillings a day!

In the long hot summer days we stacked oats, wheat and barley, getting scratches on our bare arms and legs from the stubble and the sheaves. The barley and thistles were worse. We spent scorching days crouching on the ground pea picking. We were as brown as berries. Life was hard but fun.

Once when we were coming home on the 4.08, the school train from Hitchin, we were machine gunned at Wymondley with bullets crashing around us with spurts of flame. At Stevenage every head was out of the window to see what had happened. The plane had flown low along our road and over Hitchin. The incident was reported in the national press, "School train machine gunned".

Stevenage was the first staging post out of London, the next one being York. There was a tented camp hidden under the trees in Whitney Wood amongst the bluebells, where the troops would go for meals and to sleep. The lorries, coaches, tanks, guns and even the funnels for the smoke-screens on D-Day stayed overnight along our long road and under the magnificent trees in The Avenue to St Nicholas church.

One night the lorries came in, stopped and all went off again to reappear on the other side of the road. Someone had realised that they always came in and parked on the side of the road with the fire hydrants, so that if there were any bombs or fires, the firemen couldn't get to the water supply.

Often the soldiers and airmen left their vehicles and slept in people's houses. Seven or so to a house – in the chairs, on the sofas, on the floor and under the dining room table. They left the front door on the latch as they went upstairs to have a bath. It was open house! If there were air raids at night we slept downstairs on a mattress in the hallway in the well of the stairs. Some of the most terrifying attacks were the V1s, the flying bombs. You could hear them coming and prayed that their engines would not cut out. When they did, you waited with bated breath for the "bang".

One very bright, clear sunrise about six o'clock, my parents called me into their room to see trails going straight up from the horizon. These they took to be V2s being fired from Holland.

Once there was a military exercise around the country. You could hear the rattle of the machine-gun fire. There was an anti-aircraft gun in the field, by the pillbox on the corner of our road. My father took up buckets of hot water for them to shave and promised more in the morning. These he took to find the field empty. They had fled! I remember dog fights overhead and the sky thick with planes towing gliders before the D-Day landings.

One afternoon we were caught in an air raid at Hitchin

swimming pool and watched the planes go over to bomb Vauxhall at Luton. We could see the smoke rising from the air raid.'

DOING OUR BIT

Many of us served our country at home, whether it was in the Women's Land Army or the Home Guard. 'Dad's Army' has had to put up with a great deal of mirth at its expense over the years, but the bravery of the men who prepared every night to defend their homes and families against what seemed like imminent invasion should never be forgotten.

THE LAND GIRLS

'In about 1942 I joined a group of London office-workers to become a land girl for a week, living under canvas. We were to spend the daytime helping a farmer to stook his corn at Little Hay.

I remember being fairly useless and not feeling I was helping the farmer, so my friend and I walked away across the moor, through Hemel Hempstead and out to Piccotts End Mill Youth Hostel. A fairly elderly couple were in charge; you heard rats or mice running around when in bed and you washed in the pond outside, but had a super breakfast of marmalade made to go further with rhubarb, and home-made haricot beans in tomato to replace the non-existent baked beans.'

'When in the spring of 1944, I arrived as a land girl in the village of Westmill, near Buntingford, little did I know that nearly 50 years on I would still be living here to recall those far off days.

I came from a town knowing little of village life and those first years here were a revelation to me and became firmly imprinted on my memory.

The village then was a busy place, the local farmers employed many men, and they were always to be seen about the street, with their horses and carts or bringing in the cows. The village shop did a brisk trade and it was here that the housewives would gather to catch up on the local gossip. Westmill was also lucky in that it had some local industry. The Herts Woodworking Company owned

The land army girls were an essential part of farm life during the war and for many it proved an enjoyable and rewarding experience. (Photograph courtesy of Hitchin Museum)

by Mr Charles Hummerstone employed about a dozen men who made some of the best ladders in England and supplied many of the big London stores. They were also the local undertakers and in this capacity made coffins as well as directing the funerals.

The butchers from neighbouring Buntingford called twice a week, the baker every day and on Monday the "oil man" would come from Braughing delivering paraffin and hardware. He sometimes brought Madeira cake and jam tarts, which in those days of rationing were quickly snapped up despite their marked flavour of paraffin. This obliging gentleman also delivered the Sunday papers, the daily ones coming from Buntingford.

The milk for the village was supplied from the local pub The Sword in Hand and from Gaylor's Farm where I lived and was employed. The milk was mostly supplied from the can and needless to say rationing was not strictly adhered to. The pub in those days was small with no pumps at all, the beer carried from the cellar by jug. The combination of beer and milk was hard work for Mr Jackson the landlord who had to start the day early with the milking and finish late with refreshments for the locals.

Very few houses sported bathrooms, and most folk had to manage with a bungalow bath in front of the fire. Westmill, however, was forward thinking and installed a bathroom in the village hall and here for the sum of sixpence one was able, after first informing the caretaker of the village hall, to wallow in piping hot water.

The village abounded with local characters, such as the crusty old colonel who insisted on being addressed by his rank. He constantly waged war with the local children who played cricket on the green in front of his house. He was somewhat eccentric, always wore his army puttees and had been known to shoot at overhead enemy aircraft, while still in his pyjamas. Over the years he owned a succession of wirehaired terriers, each one called Mr Pinch. In a small bungalow lived twin sisters straight out of Jane Austen, about 70 years of age, one timid and sweet, the other autocratic. The village school was ruled by Mrs McKinnie, an excellent teacher with an absorbing passion for rabbits, and the children spent many an hour collecting food for them and cleaning out their hutches.

My life at the farm was hard work but how I loved it. In common with most dwellings at that time, there was no hot water, and the copper fuelled by sticks was kept going all day, the first one up in the morning lighting it. I often experienced some difficulty getting it to ignite and one morning resorted to using paraffin. The flames promptly blew outwards, burning off my eyebrows and singeing the tails of the three cats sleeping on the top for warmth.

I shall never forget the wonderful food we had there, cream, home-made butter (which took us hours to make with the glass churn) and on my first morning I was asked how many pork chops I would like for breakfast!

The cows were milked by hand, the chickens were all running free, and the pigs were kept in warm beds of straw with a large open yard to run in. In the spring a handsome shire stallion bedecked with ribbons and jingling brass visited the village in order to effect marriages with mares who had romance on their minds. The corn was cut with a binder and the shandy we drank out of a bottle on top of a half built stack could have been nectar.

The whist drives held in the village hall were well attended, the prizes being mostly rabbits, eggs and potatoes. The WI meetings were concerned mainly with 'Make do and Mend' and how to make a little go a long way, but all the ladies went, there were few nights out for them.

The little station with its white picket fence, shining brass and colourful flowerbeds was the meeting place for many travellers who gathered in the station master/porter/ticket collector's office. The waiting room was never used, folk much preferred the warmth from the stove and the smell of breakfast that was usually being fried about 7.30am in this immaculately kept little room. A cheap day return to Liverpool Street was then about one shilling and tenpence. What happy memories.'

THE WVS

'After I qualified in 1944, I got my first job and came to St Albans. I joined the WVS and worked one evening a week in the Services Canteen, which was held in the Market Hall behind St Peter's Street. Being new, I started off on the washing-up, (no detergent washing-up liquid then!) but then graduated to the cooking. We must have made other things, but all I can remember were omelettes, made with dried egg, hundreds of cheese omelettes, or "ham" omelettes made with Spam and all served with baked beans and chips.

I was lucky enough to get essential petrol coupons for my job, and as there was no basic petrol ration at the time I had to fill in the forms and state the exact mileage and my route from the garage in Catherine Street where I kept the car to each destination, and woe betide me if I was ever caught off my route! I daren't even drive back to my digs.

To save our clothing coupons, we used to buy darning wool if we could get it, and with a two-ply knitting pattern knit jumpers. I also remember knitting bedroom slippers with rug wool and then sewing them onto a sole. Once at a department store, I bought a fawn blanket (no coupons) and at their suggestion went to the household linen department to buy a tablecloth (no coupons) for the lining, and a dressmaker made me a very warm cosy dressing gown, which lasted years! When I got married, my mother was given a silk parachute, and made me some silk "cami-knicks".

One day in the June of that year, it was a lovely warm sunny day and I sat on the green outside the Abbey to eat my lunch. As I and many others ate our sandwiches, there was a dull roar and the sky became filled with huge planes, each one towing a glider. They were filled with troops, and flew fairly low over the Abbey, and they seemed to go on for ever.

We realised that it was D-Day and the invasion of Normandy had begun. It made such an impact on me, that even to this day every time I walk down Abbey Mill Lane, past the spot where I sat that day, I see the sky black with planes and gliders flying over the Abbey.'

THE HOME GUARD

'The Second World War was in full swing and I was just about to enter the junior school. My memories of those cold winter days are very vague but I can remember being met at the school gate by my mother, who said my brother and I were to be very quiet when we got home as my father was asleep, and that he had been awake all the previous night. This is the story as Dad told it to me. Home Guard duty that night had been spent at Park Street, near St Albans (where we lived) and instructions were to guard the Handley Page aerodrome, runway and aircraft factory. For several hours, through the darkest part of the night, an aircraft could be heard overhead, circling round and round . . . unsure if the aircraft was friend or foe, the Home Guard continued duty in darkness and silence.

At first light, a roaring rumbling sound neared – to reveal a Lancaster bomber attempting a crash landing. It overshot the runway, crashed through farm buildings into a hay rick, coming to rest in a pig sty, the squealing animals adding to the terrifying sound. Dad and his fellow Home Guard members ran as fast as they could towards the wreckage to assist the seven man crew of the bomber. The pilot, having miraculously freed himself and in a state of shock was found wandering amid the turmoil. Dad's first aid expertise, for which he had several medals, came to the fore as they freed five of the crew. The emergency services then arrived on the scene and immediately dealt with the release of the gunner who was trapped and suffering from multiple injuries. All seven crew members were transferred to hospital in St Albans. Dad and his colleagues continued to stand guard over the wreckage amid dead and dying animals. Farm sewage and the hay was saturated with leaking fuel – until eventually the RAF arrived on the scene to take charge and allow the Home Guard to go off duty. Exhausted, my father arrived home, having first reported the reason for his absence from work as a plumber on the LMS railway, to the office, only to find at the end of the week, one day's pay deducted from his wage packet.

The pilot of the Lancaster bomber made a full recovery and wrote a letter of thanks to the Home Guard. It became evident that the aircraft had been on a night raid over Germany and had received severe damage. The pilot flew it homeward, having lost radio contact, and with the loss of the instrument panel. He was unaware of his where-abouts in England and so had circled using his remaining fuel, awaiting daybreak, when he happened to spy the Handley Page airfield, and prepared for an emergency landing.'

'My father, Frank Edwards at 41 years was over age for the army, so he joined the Home Guard at Northchurch along with four others in our road, including the civil engineer who was billeted with us as he worked for a firm evacuated from London. None was in the habit of going to the pub but on Tuesday nights after Home Guard that's where they ended up, at The Crooked Billet. They all rode bicycles which often got stolen by soldiers who were in the barracks at Ashridge. They rode the bikes back to barracks and then threw them in the bracken on the common.

Circa 1941. Alarm! Parachutists seen dropping on Northchurch Common! Were they German? The Home Guard was called out and they rushed up to the common on their bikes. Wives became very anxious, especially after several hours missing their tea! Our next door neighbour Mrs Rigby (no one ever called the neighbours by their Christian names then) announced that she was taking "Len" some sandwiches for his tea because he must be famished up there on the common. Incidentally, the parachutists turned out to be two British airmen bailing out of a damaged plane.

The commanding officer was Mr Dixon, a Berkhamsted vet. He taught his section how to make a raft of old oilcans lashed together so that they could cross the canal. The raft was built but no one would venture on to it. Mr Dixon said he would do it – "Safe as houses", he said, and climbed aboard. They let the rope out until the raft was mid-canal where it's deep. He began to sink slowly and said, "Pull me in!" but they all laughed so much that no-one pulled him in and he sank! I remember hearing those men come home on that summer evening pushing their bikes up the hill and laughing and laughing!

During the war we were the only house in Meadow Road, Berkhamsted who had a telephone and that was because my father was a chauffeur and his boss had it installed so that he could call him in emergencies. No one could get a telephone installed so everyone in the road used ours. We knew all the neighbours' secrets – but some terrible tragedies also came via that telephone because of the war. Out of the 23 houses in the road, ten men were in the armed forces and two were killed. One message that came regularly was for Mr Cox, the fireman

205

at the bottom of the road – to tell him that either the "Yellow Light is showing" (he must stand by) or "Red light is showing (enemy aircraft approaching) or "Purple light is showing" (get his skates on because Berkhamsted has enemy aircraft overhead)! Life was very busy even if only running the messages.'

RATIONS AND MAKING DO

'Making do' – what memories those two words conjure up of hand-me-down clothes, dull food and all the irksome restrictions of shortages and rationing. If we saw a queue we joined it, in the hope there would be something good at the end of it! Though recycling has become something of a modern phenomenon, many of us became extremely good at it during the war years.

JOIN THE QUEUE

'Little thought on my part then was given to the difficulties my mother (and thousands of others) were having in feeding us on war-time rations, but I cannot remember ever feeling deprived or going hungry. It was a joke that if you saw a food queue you joined it even if you didn't know what you were queuing for! Like many of our neighbours, we kept chickens and Dad grew most of our own vegetables. "Digging for Victory" was a slogan of the time. We also tried keeping rabbits to eke out the meat ration but we made pets of them, gave them names and not one of them ever ended up on our plates. We also had a share in a pig. At one period of the war Dad was stationed at the caddie house at Oxhey Golf Links and he and his fellow firemen kept this pig round the back, which was fed on scraps and at a later date we had our share of bacon and pork.

Clothes coupons didn't go very far and it was a case of make do and mend. I can still remember quite a few of my dresses etc from that period because I wore them so many times. Oh, the thrill of owning my first pair of nylons! These were so precious that if you got a ladder you took them to a little lady in Market Street, Watford, who carefully picked up the stitches with a tiny hook and invisibly mended runs at about a shilling or one and sixpence each.

How much safer our towns were after dark when I was growing up, even in war time when there were no lights and a bicycle lamp or torch had to have most of the glass covered with black paper, leaving just a pencil beam of light. Many a time I cycled from Watford Town Hall late at night after a dance back to Oxhey or came out of the cinema to catch the last bus home at 10.30pm. Our only fears then were being accosted by a drunk or being wolf-whistled by a GI!'

'The only good thing I can remember that came out of the war was the food parcels that came to our village from Essendon in Australia. The link was a man called Richard Green, who had lived at the mill and who had emigrated from our Essendon to found a city of the same name on the other side of the world.

We all had to go to the vicarage where the parcels were given out. Quantity depended on the size of the family. Mother always said these were a godsend because of the food shortages and rationing. They contained tins of fruit, jam, dripping etc. The children also had gifts of sweets and chocolate. For these we had to go to another large house, Essendon Place, which was owned by Lord and Lady Essendon. Each child had a shoebox-sized parcel of hard boiled sweets and wonderful bars of chocolate. We will always be grateful to the Australian Essendon.'

'I remember the milkman and his dog at Barnet. Yes, he did have a horse too, and my mother sent me to follow it with a bucket and shovel. During the war when milk was rationed, many wives and mothers in the neighbourhood joined the black market in a small way and gave the milkman a "tip" weekly so that they would get any surplus pints. Our milkman spent his ill-gotten gains on buying a greyhound to make his fortune on the track and – hurrah for natural justice – it died!'

'During the Second World War, when many things were in short supply, we had a wonderful barter system at Hertingfordbury. It was held at the local school, known

Food parcels from Essendon, Australia reach Essendon in Hertfordshire during the Second World War.

locally as Birch Green school. Points were awarded for each garment brought in, shoes or whatever, and could be exchanged for something of equal points value.

It worked very well, no money was involved and nothing was wasted. Many people found it a boon for saving clothing coupons for other items which would have been impossible to get, as coupons were not plentiful.'

'During the war I worked at Waltham Cross post office. I became pregnant and had a craving for potato crisps. They were almost unobtainable and like gold dust. One day when I was working behind the counter, a young lady came in with two packets of crisps on the top of her basket. I must have been looking longingly at them and almost drooling when suddenly she said, "Would you like a packet of crisps? I can see by your face you would" and she passed me a packet over the counter. I was surprised and so grateful and will never forget her kind gesture. It's the little things that make such happy memories, even in the most troublesome times.'

'During the war we had evacuees of all shapes and sizes at our house in Berkhamsted, and the living room table was our shelter during air raids at night. We used to listen to the doodlebugs going over and wait for the bang, and watched the searchlights looking for German planes.

As a family we went wooding; taking an old pram to collect the wood and having a picnic as well. Food rationing didn't make a lot of difference to us; we grew all our own vegetables, kept chickens, ducks and rabbits. I also remember going out rabbiting with my dad. He would set the wires one day and we'd go back the next day to see if we had caught anything. He'd go pigeon shooting too, he had several wooden decoys to attract the live ones down into the field.'

'In Berkhamsted Co-op they used to pat the butter and slice the bacon on demand. I remember a small boy pushing a large, deep baby's pram up to the counter. It was empty except for a pile of ration books, probably a dozen. The assistant laboriously marked every page on every book and filled the pram with all the rations for a very large family.

One cold Saturday morning I queued for hours at Lintott's in Berkhamsted for the usual pound of sausages. I fainted with the cold.'

AND AFTER THE WAR

'Wartime memories include trundling the wheelbarrow to the gas works to get a sack of coke for the kitchen boiler, and being told they had "blended" chocolate at the sweet shop and rushing there on my bicycle. This was before sweet rationing which at least meant fair shares for all. I remember the baker's shop where I was told, "No fruit cake today – your mother had one last week." Fruit cake! It had about six currants in it.

Wartime "make do and mend" meant having to wear my sister's clothes cut down to fit. We saved everything – paper bags, bits of string, elastic etc. My mother hoarded precious tins of fruit for Christmas and birthdays and if lucky, a tin of Nestles cream. We were lucky – we had relatives in Canada and got a food parcel every year.

Bassingbourne aerodrome was not far away and every weekend Baldock was "invaded" by American servicemen, who to us children seemed so fascinating. I remember standing in our back garden many afternoons watching wave after wave of "Flying Fortresses" going over on bombing raids in Germany.

After the war shortages seemed to be even worse – how my mother coped I don't know. My sister got married in 1952 and because she bought her sheets and blankets at our local shop she was allowed to buy two pairs of nylons!

I worked at ICI in Welwyn Garden City at about that time and we were all given three pairs of stockings to wear and test. We later found out they were the first to be made from "Terylene", ICI's new wonder fibre. Rationing went on till 1954 – finishing, thankfully, just before I got married in September of that year.'

RECYCLING AS A WAY OF LIFE

'Re-cycling was a commonplace activity in our home when I was a small child during the Second World War. In fact it was a challenge to my father to find a potential re-use for almost anything left over or thrown out. He was employed during the war years as a woodwork and metal-work master at the secondary school in Ware. He and the Domestic Science teacher shared an annexe building opposite the public swimming pool, some ten minutes walk from the main school. For Dad, of course, it was of paramount importance to acquire sufficient wood for use in school. Even the glue he used was obtained from boiled-down bones he collected from the bone-tins fastened to the lamp posts around the town. He begged and scrounged any odd bits of wood he could from local wood yards and industries. Any scrap, however small, could be used, even rough tea chests begged from grocers' shops. Someone offered him a stack of thin, three inch wide planks. He carefully glued and clamped them side by side until they were wide enough to make into doors for the built-in wardrobe he was constructing in his bedroom.

The local rubbish dump was a valuable source of challenge and inspiration. One find was a messy box of discarded ball-point pens, something we had never seen before. They were all in parts, mostly broken, and ink leaking all over the place. Mum was not amused by his attempts to clean them up in the kitchen. A few were eventually usable, and presentable once the barrels had been polished on his lathe. I remember when I was very tiny struggling to reach the pedals of a gleaming red pedal car I had been given for my birthday. Years later I learnt that Dad had found it on the dump, a badly battered and broken wreck.

Another toy I loved very much, which of course had come from the woodwork room, was Dobbin, a sit-on or push-along horse, I believe it was my main walking aid as a toddler. Dad sanded down a wooden vegetable box, attached ropes, and it became my first swing. At the age of four he gave me a bundle of balsa wood pieces and a sharp jack-knife. My grandfather was furious and said he was crazy. Dad replied that I would soon learn which was the sharp side of the blade and anyway a blunt instrument usually inflicts a far deeper wound than a sharp one – I learnt. Very soon I had made crude little boats to float in the bath, and before long learnt to use a hack-saw, and produced more presentable toys.

My sewing skills I learnt from my mother. At the end of our road a factory, then called "Ware-rite" produced fabric for covering the fuselage of wooden framed aircraft. A jubilant dad came home with armfuls of off-cuts of this fabric, as stiff as boards and with an unpleasant smell from the powdery yellow dressing. After a week or two of soaking in the bath to dissolve the dressing, and then a good boil, my mother had a good supply of beautifully soft beige linen-like material, ideally suitable for many different things. Dad went back for more. Several pretty tray cloths and cushion covers were embroidered, and practical items such as aprons and curtains appeared from Mum's sewing machine. I soon learnt to use a needle, and help with the embroidery. I then went on to doll making with my closest friend. We each made a pair of six inch high twins from old lock-knit cotton vests suitably dyed flesh colour by our mothers. For several years we

212

designed and made "fashion" clothes for them from scraps of materials, until we progressed to making our own clothes.

A challenge for Mum came with the arrival of a bundle of pieces of white parachute silk, each narrow panel cut on the bias. However, she and a group of friends produced an amazing number of blouses and pretty items of lingerie. There was a School of Dancing in the town, which had in the past had a uniform of a white poplin blouse and short black satin skirt. By the time I joined during the war, we all wore skirts made of window black-out material, and blouses fashioned from the best parts of worn-out cotton sheets. We were never short of costumes for our performances in pantomimes and concerts, such were the skills of our mothers.

Our church Christmas Bazaars sold many goods made by my parents; Mum's sewing and of course Dad's wooden items; dishes, bowls and always several trays of various sizes, the edges wound round with brightly coloured cane, and I helped to bind them. Mum's tray is still in daily use, 50 years on, and looking like new. A factory producing electrical wiring had given Dad a quantity of variously coloured rubber insulation casings. My friends and I had to plait them onto hair grips, which were sold in matching pairs on pieces of card. Very soon my friends and I had very fashionable hair accessories. The toy stalls were well stacked with pull-along toys and dolls house furniture, with Mum's help in making little cushions and other soft furnishings from scraps of fabric. With the use of a jig-saw, a three inch length of one by one inch wood was transformed into a cleverly interlocking table, two chairs and two stools for dolls houses. Long before I thought I had out-grown my most precious picture book, Dad took it and mounted each page onto board, and within a frame cut them into jig-saw puzzles. As a consolation I was given back my favourite page, but with the irritation of having to put the puzzle together before appreciating the picture, and for me it was spoilt.

My father's was a Reserved Occupation, so he was not called up. He and some other teachers joined the Air Training Corps, and flew small aircraft from Panshanger airfield, spending much of their spare time there, but they never flew in battle. Forever looking for discarded items, Dad found a chipped search-light lens, he had it silvered and it is still to this day serving as a magnifying mirror in the bathroom. A damaged nose wheel from a Mosquito aircraft came his way, and gave a new lease of life to his wheelbarrow.

Possibly the greatest achievement was a clinker-built rowing boat for four oarsmen Dad made with his school-boys. Most of the wood came from the wreck of a Hurricane bomber. They used it on the river Lea, launched from a quay close to the annexe. He always told the lock-keeper before going on the water. One day tragedy struck, he found the lock-keeper face down in the lock, having fallen from his dinghy. Dad immediately stopped rowing on the river until each boy had passed a swimming test. With the blessing of the swimming pool attendant, he had free access to the pool to train and test the boys. He made diving bricks, made from wooden blocks with a hole in each filled with lead, and got them to swim through hoops below the surface. Finally they were trained in life saving. From this necessary safety precaution, developed the Watermanship swimming tests now used by the County for junior aged children. I was taught to swim with confidence long before I reached school age, Dad said it was far more important than learning the three R's, which could come later.

By the end of the war, I was an avid reader and loved Enid Blyton's "Fives" and "Adventure" series, and also all the adventures written by Malcolm Saville and Arthur Ransome, and Captain John's "Biggles" and "Worralls" series. I frequently had my bedside light-bulb removed when I abused the lights out rule. What else could I do when every chapter ended in a cliff hanger? Torch batteries were too expensive and used all my pocket money, so I used initiative. Dad had taken empty powdered milk tins, drilled a small hole each side, and put a low watt electric light bulb inside each. Mum made covers from old woollen coats and we all had electric bed warmers. Here was a source of light – I read under the covers!'

MUSIC IN THE DARK DAYS

'For a year I stayed with my parents in Ware during the Second World War. By a lucky chance I met Joan Singleton, a pianist who had accompanied Joan Hammond, a renowned soprano. With her great friend Aline Hay, who lived in Thundridge, she often visited WIs to give an afternoon's music. Joan, having invited me to sing in a concert in Ware parish church in aid of what we all referred to as "plucky little Finland", asked me to join them.

Once we had to wait in Ware until the all clear sounded before setting out for some distant village. The members waiting there just went on knitting till we arrived. The knitting didn't stop when we started the concert. I remember so often singing to a hall full of tops of heads and the click, click of needles. That is why to this day, one of the rules for our County Music Festivals is "no knitting permitted in the hall".

Another very cold afternoon, we arrived at a small village and were dismayed to see an apparently empty hall. That was until we realised the audience were all huddled round two lukewarm radiators at the side. Miss Hay was the violinist of the party. She was a friend of Jelly d'Aranyi, who often stayed with friends, Mr and Mrs Fletcher who had bought Sacombe House from the Hay family. I remember a wonderful private concert there to which Aline kindly invited me. I had last seen Jelly d'Aranyi in York Minster standing in a spotlight high in the organ loft. The singer was Elena Gerhart, also a friend of Mrs Fletcher's and already at the top of her profession. It was a magical evening and in wartime too!

Aline Hay kept a diary of her visits to WIs in which she not only gave the programme, numbers in the audience etc, she also noted which dress she wore. With clothes rationing and small children to clothe, I only had one "singing dress".

On looking back at those war years, it is as if the dark days brought out an expression of hope and even greater strength. There was drama, music, and painting in every WI, as well as preserving, bottling, collecting chestnuts and rose hips.'

WARTIME ROMANCE

Even in the darkest days of the war, or perhaps then more than ever, romance still flourished. Boy met girl who might otherwise never have known of each other's existence and the dangers of war made each day very precious. With separation a certainty, marriages were quickly arranged and joyously celebrated, despite the difficulties.

LOVE AND MARRIAGE

'When war broke out in 1939, I was 13 years old. My memories of wartime include filling sandbags to help protect Hertford County Hospital and going to the Food Office to write names and addresses on ration books. In October 1940, I spent two weeks in the County Hospital after an appendix operation.

This was of course during the blitz. Every night an enamel wash bowl was left on the bed table. The first night, I asked the nurse what it was for – it was to put on my head to protect myself from flying glass. Fortunately, although there were bombs most nights, the bowl wasn't needed.

About 1942, just before I left school, the corvette HMS Guillemot was adopted by the school. The girls made up parcels to send to the ratings on the ship. Each parcel had a number on it and when they arrived in Harwich where the ship was based, the ratings had a number given to them. The parcel which my youngest sister and her friend had made up was "won" by AB Jim Johnston. As he lived in Belfast, he couldn't always get home for short leaves. My mother invited him to spend a few days with us, and the rest you might say is history. It was love at first sight for both of us, and in 1946 we were married.

One other deep memory of wartime, is when a "doodlebug" fell into the river Lea one Sunday morning. As I was a telephone operator, I was called to go on duty. The devastation on Mill Bridge was terrible, but fortunately the bridge itself was not damaged. A handbag shop near the bridge was blown to bits and people had a grand time fishing handbags from the river.'

'In Hunsdon there was an aerodrome for the wartime planes, bringing 1,500 airmen to the sleepy little village. The local boys didn't get a chance.'

'We moved to St Albans when I was 18. It was a delightful little country market town and I found plenty of social life. I met my future husband at a dance. We enjoyed those dances – we did not need alcohol and it was not allowed anyway; it was all so romantic to dance the waltz, foxtrot and quickstep with a smartly dressed young man who would walk one home afterwards. We were engaged when the war started and like so many other young men he volunteered for the army straight away. He joined the Grenadier Guards and was in training at Chelsea Barracks, so for the first few months he was able to travel to St Albans at weekends to see me. He was eventually posted to Windsor, and during a seven day leave we talked about getting married. Life was so uncertain by then and he would be going abroad at any time. He found that he was only entitled to five days leave to get married, and was told he would have to take the leave offered as the battalion would be going abroad and it was now or never.

He called me on the phone and said, "We are getting married next weekend OK?" I mumbled a few words about it being short notice and remember putting the phone down and being rooted to the spot wondering how I was going to arrange everything in a week, and how to break the news to my parents. The news was received in stunned silence – I was their only child and their reaction was one of disappointment that I could not possibly have a proper wedding arranged within a week. However, I was in love and it was wartime so I had to start thinking! I wanted a church service so I had to see the Dean of St Albans Abbey to obtain a special licence.

He promised to try to obtain it in time for the wedding service which was arranged for 2.30pm on 4th May 1940 at St Michael's church. I then had to think about what I would be able to wear – I did not have enough clothing coupons for a wedding dress even if one had been obtainable, austerity was the keyword of our existence then. I bought a practical dress and jacket which I wore for special occasions until the end of the war. We were determined to make the most of our five days and have a short honeymoon, and we were very lucky to have friends who rallied round and lent us a car and collected petrol coupons. The day before the wedding I felt drained – I had to buy my own wedding ring and even order my flowers. The car had been left at a neighbour's house with the wedding certificate, the ring and a note on the front seat so that my husband-to-be would not see me on the morning of the wedding.

The service was perfect with just our parents and a few friends and relations present. My mother had managed to prepare a light lunch – no wedding cake, but we did have two bottles of champagne – we saved one for when the war ended. We spent three days touring in Sussex, the weather was glorious but we did have difficulty in finding bed and breakfast. My husband was in his Guards uniform and we were eyed very suspiciously by the first landlady who said, "No, not for one night!" My mother had warned us to take our marriage certificate with us, but we felt really guilty at this reaction. When we returned home my mother had turned my bedroom into a comfortable bed-sitter and this was to be our home for the duration.

Three years went by – very uncertain years of partings and meetings. I still held my job in the retail food trade which kept me from being conscripted into a factory, but the powers-that-be were catching up on me. By the time I became pregnant my employer had run out of excuses to keep me, even though I was doing all the paperwork and counting food coupons etc.

A month before my son was born, my husband was sent abroad and we did not see him for three years. He did not know for six weeks after the birth that he was a father. He was on the high seas at the time so I had no address to write to.

My baby was born in Diocesan House, St Albans, which had been turned into a maternity hospital for the York Road Lying-in Hospital in London. The trouble was it was not properly equipped, and the nurses had to carry buckets of water up two flights of stairs. In the early morning we were awakened with a cup of tea, the baby yelling to be fed, and a bowl of water to wash – all at the same time. We had very little sleep as tanks and army vehicles of all kinds were rumbling past. They were made at Vauxhall Motors in Luton and were on their way to unknown destinations.

We had to stay in hospital for a fortnight in those days and our bed linen was only changed once as laundries were non-existent. The Sisters were like Victorian harridans – the poor nurses had to "bob" and say, "Reporting for duty, Sister" at the office before they started a shift. The food was appalling and the worst thing of all was having to express our surplus milk into a basin every night to supply babies who were unable to have their mother's milk.

The next three years were grim – my husband was in Italy and the war was really terrible, but life went on in a peculiar uncertain way. Every night we could hear the ack-ack guns and see the reflection of the flames of the blitz in London. Thank goodness St Albans escaped that kind of horror – although we did have a few bombs and missiles. We endured two very severe winters and it gave us satisfaction then to see German prisoners of war shovelling the snow and emptying the dustbins.

At last it was over and we settled in St Albans for over 40 years.'

HIGHDAYS & HOLIDAYS

MAKING YOUR OWN
ENTERTAINMENT

In the days before television and other instant entertainment, people got together in clubs and societies in their towns or villages to create their own social life. Plays, concerts, sports – there was something to appeal to everyone, and a wealth of talent lay hidden within even the quietest community.

FROM SHAKESPEARE TO CRICKET

'At Little Munden before the First World War entertainment was varied. There was an annual school concert, a Men's Club where darts, billiards, dominoes and cards were weekly events, cricket, football, bell ringing, magic lantern shows and a Band of Hope for the youngsters. In 1918 our WI was formed and we flocked to join – two shillings and sixpence annual subscription. Now we had something of our own. All these activities took place in a confined space and much improvisation was necessary to make larger events possible.

I must add that special evenings were always fixed according to the Parish Lantern, ie the full moon. This was most important.'

'Country dance parties were often held at Redbourn in the 1920s and on one occasion a harmonium was pushed onto the common so that Miss Apthorpe could play the music for dancing. Dancing round the maypole was an annual event and girls spent the previous days collecting material from the hedges and gardens to make their garlands.

Shakespeare was once performed under a widely spreading tree in Redbourn House garden, and clowns performed in the High Street to raise money for the hospital.'

'When there was no village hall in Park Street, everything happened in Dr Gilby's room, from meetings of the WI to the Cricket Supper. He was a lovely old man, always smiling and kind. We had a cricket match one year, Ladies vs the Frogmore Cricket Club.'

'I was fortunate to be living in Oxhey in the 1930s, an area where there were many young people around my own age. We had a youth club and an amateur dramatic society, both held in the hall of our local church of St Francis, plus a flourishing community centre which opened up at the end of the war. Between them they provided all the entertainment and activities we needed, bonding friendships which have lasted to the present day. We did things in a group – cycling to Windsor, swimming in the old gravel pit at Hampermill, going to dances and learning to ice skate at Richmond Ice Rink and later at Wembley when it reopened after the war.'

'At Bayford we had a village youth club (post war), and we often played other villages at billiards and table tennis. Eventually we had Girl Guides. We graduated to whist and social evenings with refreshments – but no alcohol, followed by dancing and games. Bayford had a football team and of course, cricket. On a Sunday the whole village would take a picnic to the cricket ground and cheer Bayford on. Once a year the team played the WI and my mother was the wicket keeper. Those were the days when cricket had its supporters!'

'Fancy dress parties were very popular at Essendon in the 1940s, held at the village hall. Not only the children dressed up but the adults as well. Anything you wanted from a hat for a funeral to a pair of cricket trousers or a pair of football boots, go to Lally Hagger, queen of the jumble sales, and she could fit you out. She had a heart of gold. We also had old time dancing once a week in the hall run by Mr Onion. My favourite was the Eva Three Step danced with my cousin, and his black patent shoes and the white powder put all over the floor. What happy days.'

'The oldest hall in Welham Green is the Men's Institute, and flower shows used to be held there along with whist drives. The flower show is now held in the Youth Centre, with other activities. Beyond the Gilethorpe Arms pub in Station Road, there used to be a large wooden building with a stage in front where open air concerts were held. We children were encouraged to go up on the stage and sing a song, with a prize for the best singer. One of the songs we had to sing was *I'm lazy, lazy*. What fun it was. No sound came from some of us when we tried to sing!'

'As a group of girls in our teens in the early 1950s, we used to go from Berkhamsted to the Old Time Dances at the Ovaltine factory and at Watford Town Hall and catch the last train home around midnight. Then with boy-friends we would walk up across the common to Potten End. We were only allowed out this late when we went dancing, otherwise we all had to be home between ten and half past.'

'In the late 1930s I often used to go to the dances at The Cherry Tree, Welwyn Garden City, walking home late to Lemsford afterwards. I was never frightened of being on my own, except passing the river where there were water rats about.'

'In the early 1950s the Co-operative Society organised an event on the Oxhey playing fields for members' children. We had games and races, country dancing and a sing-song. Each child paid one shilling and sixpence and received a brown paper bag containing a paste sandwich, a fairy cake and a third of a pint bottle of orange juice for their tea. Entertainment was far less sophisticated in those days.'

LEARNING TO SWIM

No chlorinated swimming baths for the children of the first half of the century, they learned to swim in the river and had great fun doing so – despite the dangers of swallowing a tadpole from time to time.

FISH BETWEEN OUR TOES

'My father came from an Oxhey/Bushey family in the 1910s. There were five children in the family and they all learned to swim at the Five Arches Bathing Place, which was actually part of the river Colne where the banks had been widened. Bathing huts and a diving board were provided. One lady was put off swimming there "because she could feel the fish swimming between her feet".'

'We all learned to swim in the early 1920s; it was a main sport and we belonged to the Victoria Swimming Club in the river Lea. We actually swam in the river and the pool for beginners was river water also. We cycled or walked

Swimming in Hertfordshire's rivers, such as the river Lea at Mill Green, was a popular sport.

the mile each way to the river from our home on the Hertfordshire/Middlesex border. We had an annual gala with swimming races in the river, and enjoyed a free cup of Bovril afterwards.'

'We had a swimming pool in the 1920s, but it was always called "the swimming or bathing river" and was a dammed stretch of the river Lea. It was down the Hertford Road from Digswell, or over the fields by Bull Stag Green and where now is the Ryde housing estate, to the hamlet of Mill Green. There behind the millwheel house was this lovely section of the river. There was always a good current flowing which made it more exciting. There was a low springboard and huts – Boys and Girls being spaced well apart! Everybody enjoyed this spot and the banks were lined with all ages of spectators who came to watch the fun.'

'At the age of three in 1929, I was taken by my elder sisters to the old swimming pool at Hartham. The river had been widened and the water was filtered (sometimes). I fell in the deep end and was only just saved from drowning, which gave me a lifelong fear of the water. There was no pool in Hertford as I was growing up so I never had a chance to overcome the fear.'

'I remember weekends at Chapmore End at the end of the 1940s when my father taught me to swim. He, my mother and I used to catch the bus from Broxbourne where we lived to Ware station. There we took a single-decker bus to Chapmore End. The small lake fed by a river was situated across a field and approached by walking along the top of a small waterfall where the river was on two levels. If the surface was slippery from river weed and algae we used to scratch it with stones to make a better grip.

I was about seven years old at the time. I had a swimming ring which I put round my waist to start with before I had the confidence to have a go without it. My father, who was unable to go into the water as he had suffered from TB as a young man, demonstrated the breaststroke from the bank and watched my efforts with heaps of encouragement and praise. I remember the water was always within my depth and I would boldly splash out with both arms, feet off the bottom, kicking like mad, eyes open and under the water most of the time, as I made for the bank. And I did it! I learned to swim.

Occasionally a party of young boys accompanied by adults would come and take a swim. They were from a local reform school I believe. On one such occasion they had the task of removing a wasps' nest from the river bank. You can bet we gave them a wide berth. We were fascinated watching them from the opposite bank as they smoked the wasps out and then removed the nest. I had never seen a wasps' nest before, it was absolutely amazing. A real work of art, very large and very delicate.

I remember Chapmore End being quite a pretty and rural place in those days. I went back on one occasion to recapture the time of my childhood when I made such an achievement. Needless to say I got lost. I believe it is all developed now and I don't even know if I would recognise the place where I learned to swim if somebody came along and put me in the right spot!'

THEATRE, CINEMA AND TV

_⊖_

Visits to the theatre, whether to London or to our own Watford theatre, and to 'the pictures' were eagerly anticipated. Hertfordshire did, of course, have its own film making pioneer in Arthur Melbourne-Cooper and some of the very earliest films were shown in the county.

GOING TO THE THEATRE

'At the end of 1919, my father died and this made a great difference to my mother and me. She was wonderful and gave me every encouragement to continue my education and by the early 1920s I was working in an accountant's office in the city and loved it. The girls took me to their little cafe for lunch – three courses plus coffee for one shilling and sixpence. I could also link up with old school friends (also working in the city) for trips to the theatre. We would go to the gallery for one and sixpence or the pit for three shillings and sixpence.

We had a special "drill". Whoever reached the theatre first, secured enough stools (at sixpence each) for all the party, perhaps six or so. When we were all assembled, we went to one of the Lyons Corner Houses and had a jolly good meal for two and sixpence then back to the theatre queue before the old lady collected her stools (which had minded our places). Then in to see the show, programme threepence which contained a wealth of information about the actors and actresses, adverts telling you where to garage your car for three hours whilst at the show for one and sixpence and of course, pictures of lovely clothes available at the nearby West End stores for around ten guineas.

We would leave each other outside the theatre around 11pm and go our separate ways and arrive home about midnight. Our mothers did not have to worry about our safety. No one gave a thought to anything unpleasant happening.'

'Watford provided much of my entertainment as I grew up in the 1930s – dances at the Town Hall and a choice of five cinemas and one live theatre. Saturday nights we paid our shilling at the Palace Theatre box office and then raced up the steps to try and get in the first row of the "Gods", which consisted of rows of steps with the sitting part covered in red plush. There were no backs to lean on. What marvellous value we got at this lovely old repertory theatre (now beautifully restored), seeing a different play each week and many actors and actresses who later became household names.'

AT THE PICTURES

'Although for a year or so in the late 1940s, cartoons and old Laurel and Hardy films were screened in the Brookmans Park Hotel on a Saturday morning, there has never been a cinema in Brookmans Park. To see a film it was necessary to travel into Barnet to one of the three cinemas there, or to Hatfield – where opposite Asda car park stood the old cinema, now a bingo hall, or into Potters Bar to the Ritz which was where Tesco now stands. The manager of the Ritz, Mr Frank Seymour, was always there keeping an eye on the clientele, old and young, and was a real disciplinarian feared by the teenagers – there could be no cuddling up too closely in the back row! At the end of the evening he always shook everyone by the hand as they left wishing them goodnight and a safe journey home.

However, even as early as the turn of the century,

230

going to the pictures was not an unusual experience for the people of North Mymms, and without leaving the village. The venue was a barn in the middle of a field, now covered by the houses of Sommers Road and Welham Close; it was a shelter for cattle and itinerant harvesters or potato pickers – no seats, but a child might be stood in a manger for a better view. Here some of the very first moving pictures ever made were shown by Arthur Melbourne-Cooper of St Albans, who in 1909 married a North Mymms girl who attended Water End School. Arthur Melbourne-Cooper was a pioneer in this form of entertainment and one whose name is honoured in the film world. He died in 1961.'

'Each Friday afternoon in the 1910s a Mr Richardson would cycle to Shenley from South Mimms with a magic lantern on the back of his bike. He would come to tea at our house and talk all through the meal, which we children were not allowed to do. We always had bread and butter and jam for tea and he would pile the jam up on his bread and we would stare, as this was something else we weren't allowed to do! After tea we went to the mission hall where he put on a lantern show for the children and we would all sing songs. Mr Richardson was from the London City Mission and after our harvest festival each year, the produce would be packed up and sent by train to London for distribution there.'

'We had a cinema in Digswell in the 1920s. It was held in "Priory House" which also housed the library and dance hall. Rows of chairs were put out for the occasion and a solo pianist, Mrs Sharpe, did her gallant best accompanying the films "now showing". Of course we all spurred her on during the exciting chases and fighting episodes of Charlie Chaplin, Pearl White, The Clutching Hand, and all the other early movies. But oh, the awful suspense when "to be continued" came up on the screen. How would we ever be able to wait for a whole week before we knew what happened next? In those days life and time seemed very long.'

'On Saturday afternoons in the 1920s, if Mother or Father had a few extra coppers to give us, some friends and I would catch the bus from Walkern to Stevenage. The Publics, a cinema, was the place to go and sometimes we would sit through the film twice – black and white, of course. On coming out it was either catch the bus or have a cream cake and walk home. Later when we had bicycles, we would go further out, more often to look the young lads over in Stevenage.'

'The cinema in Welwyn Garden City had a children's matinee on Saturday mornings. We would walk the mile and a half to Welwyn North station. The return fare was a penny ha'penny and it was threepence to go in the cinema.'

'The highlight of the week at Essendon in the 1940s was Friday evening, when the village hall became the local picture house. Jack would set up his projector in the little room at the back and a large screen up on stage. For sixpence we could watch a film and if you had a penny spare, you could get a bag of sweets as well.'

THE FIRST TV

'The first time I ever saw a television was in 1947 or 1948, and it was the only set in Westmill. We Sunday school children were invited into the tiny sitting room of a cottage opposite the church to watch the flickering black and white screen and see "Little Lord Fauntleroy" – no subsequent production has given such magical pleasure!'

ROYAL AND MEMORABLE OCCASIONS

⌐⊖⌐

Hertfordshire towns and villages celebrated royal jubilees and coronations with gusto, whole communities turning out to run races and dress up for parades.

THE 1930s

'I was born in Little Heath near Potters Bar. When George V died in 1936, the whole school walked the two miles to Brookmans Park to see the funeral train pass by. I don't suppose we were very impressed, but it got us out of lessons.'

'In 1935 the Sarratt Playing Fields were opened for George V's Jubilee and in 1937 trees were planted on Sarratt Green by the youngest and the oldest children in the school for George VI's Coronation.'

'In 1937 my large family was extremely poor. I wore my elder brother's boots and didn't feel too badly about it as his feet were broad and mine were narrow so my feet developed naturally. For George VI's Coronation we were to have races at school. In the practices I came last as my boots were heavy and I was thin and light. Mother decided to buy me canvas shoes for the actual day. They were lovely. I felt as light as air and won every race and was given a tiny dolly bag with a new shilling for each success.

Laden with my spoils I went to school on Monday morning, only to be hauled out and told off by the

Apsley & Nash Mills

1911.

Coronation Celebrations.

The celebrations at Apsley and Nash Mills for George V's Coronation in 1911 lasted twelve hours and ended with a torchlight procession and fireworks.

headmaster for cheating. He never thought of the boots versus canvas shoes making the difference.'

THE CORONATION IN 1953

'When my daughter broke her ankle sliding on the ice on the Hinxworth village pond, we took her for treatment to the old Lister Hospital, Hitchin. We went by way of Wilbury Hills, Letchworth, down the hill and under the railway viaduct. As we approached the viaduct a train passed over on its way to London. The windows were blacked out and it was moving extremely slowly so we had a good view. Grenadier Guards were standing on the outside of the carriage. It was the train carrying the body of George VI to his lying-in-state and burial in London. Many people lined the track and railway stations in Hertfordshire, to pay their last respects to a well loved king on his last journey from his country estate in Sandringham.'

'In 1953 Queen Elizabeth visited St Albans Abbey just prior to her Coronation. As Brown Owl I took the First Bricket Wood Brownies to see her. We all sat on the high pavements in Fishpool Street and waved and cheered as she passed.'

'I remember going to the celebrations on the football field in Hitchin for the Coronation. We were all given a present of a flat tin with a bar of chocolate and some new pennies in it. My sister being four years older than me had six pennies – I only had three!'

'In our small village we made fine creations out of "Glitterwax", a bit like plasticine but made of wax and much prettier colours, and took them to the local hospital. We went round to our neighbours on the day and, like thousands of others, crowded round a twelve inch black

235

and white television set to watch the ceremony. In the afternoon a party was held in the village hall for all the children. We had a super tea and the hall looked wonderful decked out in red, white and blue streamers and flags.'

'I was secretary of the Abbots Langley Young Farmers Club, and after we had watched the Coronation on a hired black and white television set in the village hall, we took our decorated tractor trailer in St Albans Coronation Procession. It was bitterly cold for June, but fortunately we were behind the Boy Scouts' trailer – complete with camp fire! They kept us fed on hot sausages as we blew our long coach horn through the streets.'

'Entertainments used to take place in the village hall at the Ayots, demolished when the A1(M) was built and sadly never replaced. That is where the flower and produce shows were held, since everyone had a garden and possibly an allotment too, grew their own vegetables and kept poultry. In the village hall we had our Victory party when local servicemen returned from the wars. There was also a big celebration when our present Queen was crowned, with the Countess Reventlow (relative of Barbara Hutton, the Woolworth heiress) hiring a large television set for the day to give everyone a treat.'

'At Clothall we saved our celebrations until the Saturday – a good idea as the weather was fine and not wet and cold as it was on the actual day. We made sure that every child in the village appeared in the fancy dress competition. Races for children and grown ups were held in a rather rough field and there was a bun fight in the village hall to which everyone from stately great-grandmothers to the latest baby came. We finished with a firework display to the accompaniment of oohs and aahs! It was a day to remember!'

In Shenley, as in many villages, Elizabeth II's Coronation celebrations in 1953 included a procession of decorated floats.

A SPRINKLING OF CELEBRATIONS

'There were grand celebrations in 1922 when Watford became a Borough, with a procession through the town, free cinema performances for the children, and a firework display in Cassiobury Park in the evening.'

'In the 1930s the St Nicholas Church School for Girls at Bury Mead, Stevenage, celebrated its centenary. There was a parade of the pupils through the High Street from the Stevenage Motor Company at one end, to the school at the other. I was in Mary Morrill House and carried a small banner bearing the name of the House colour ("Red") and wore a white blouse and navy knickers – I thought this very daring, being a rather shy eight year old! The three other Houses were all represented by their colour and were named after famous missionaries. A brass band led the parade and pupils and adults in Victorian costumes, with a man on a pennyfarthing bicycle, joined in.'

'When the QVM Hospital opened in Welwyn on 24th July 1934, the schoolchildren lined the drive to the hospital. It was opened by the Duchess of York, now Queen Elizabeth the Queen Mother. We all had little Union Jacks to wave. My dad was a building worker and helped to build the hospital, likewise the Welwyn Stores (now John Lewis) in Welwyn Garden City.'

FAIRS AND FEASTS

A high spot of the year was the arrival of the travelling fair, carrying on a tradition centuries old. Some fairs were derived from the old Statute Fairs, when labourers and farmworkers would be hired for the year, and were still known as 'the Statty' well into this century. Bricket Wood Fair, however, grew out of the coming of the railway at the end of the 19th century and was a tremendously popular day out for Londoners for several decades.

BRICKET WOOD FAIR

'A very happy memory of my childhood spent in Hertfordshire in the 1920s and 1930s is of listening to music coming from the fairs held on Bricket Wood Common. I lived with my parents in the neighbouring village of Park Street and on a summer's day the fairground music could be heard quite clearly in our garden.

The fair was an annual event, lasting several weeks. Parties of children from the East End of London enjoyed their Sunday school outings here and train loads of visitors would arrive at Bricket Wood station to make their way to the fairground and enjoy the swinging boats, roundabouts, coconut shies, halls of distorting mirrors, indeed all the fun of the fair, as well as a day in the country.

Very few people owned cars and I can remember ponies and traps being used to bring families from surrounding villages. Householders living en route would erect stalls to sell cut flowers, vegetables and other garden produce.

At the fairground china ornaments, similar to Goss china, showing the Herts crest and the words "Bricket Wood" could be purchased as a souvenir of a happy day spent in the Hertfordshire countryside.'

'We would walk from Abbots Langley to Bricket Wood when children in the 1920s to watch the trainloads of London factory workers arrive for the Fair. The short length of station platform meant that the train would pull along at least three times to allow all the people off. The cottagers would have been out early gathering wild foxgloves and other flowers, to sell from their doors when the crowds returned home. These cottagers also peeled rushes (withies) and made a curled type of artificial flower. I met my future wife at the Bricket Wood Fair, and I would walk to St Albans where she lived after a long day's work. There were glow worms in the lanes then, and nightingales singing in the woods as I passed.'

'I was brought up at Lye Lane, Bricket Wood over 60 years ago, when there were just a few cottages, two pubs and a chapel and the land around was mostly woods and common land. There were two fairs in the summer months. The hurdy-gurdies rattled out well known tunes of the day and the usual fairgrown attractions were there. We spent lovely days watching the children and adults arrive in thousands in trains and coaches, as so many Sunday school outings and firm's days out were sent here. It was a delight to see the East End children's faces when they saw the countryside and the wild flowers, eagerly picking them and carrying them about to take home to their parents.

My sister and I looked out each year for the Co-op day out, as they had a concert in the evening in one of the tea pavilions. We would peek through the windows to watch and they would invite us in. We also enjoyed the day when the Pearly King and Queen came, as they would have a sing-song and knees-up outside the pub while waiting for their train home.'

'The fair at Bricket Wood was full of untold delights to us children – including an ice cream cart like a little barrel on wheels. I remember charabancs driving up the lanes, filled with "outing people" and they always seemed to be singing *Horsey keep your tail up*, a song my mother didn't approve of at all.'

FAIR DAYS

'I was a child in 1920 living near the pond which in those days was in Stansted Road, Hoddesdon. We looked forward in summer to the travelling fair visiting for the Hoddesdon Fair Days 29th and 30th June. We would run up to Stanstead Road to see the steam engines go by pulling the funfair, which had to be assembled and was then driven by steam.'

'August Bank Holiday was the time of the "Statty Fair" at Hemel Hempstead, when lots of Londoners used to come by train and proceed to the local pubs and get roaring drunk, so that by nightfall the hill outside Boxmoor station was lined with people sprawled on the ground without sufficient energy to get to the station itself.

The children were given a half day holiday to attend the fair. Toffee was made by some of the women – when it was of the right consistence it was thrown back on the hook and finally twisted into shape. There was also a "spit" toffee stall, where the owner would spit on his hands before handling the sticky toffee. There were boxing booths, a shooting range, roundabouts, hoop-la, human abnormalities – all the fun of the fair and all lit by kerosene lamps and very exciting.'

A charabanc outing from Hitchin in 1913. (Photograph courtesy of Hitchin Museum)

241

'The annual Charter Fair in the 1920s was something special. It was sheer magic to smell the burnt sugar being spun into rock in the light of the naphtha flares on the stalls. Wonderful noise came from the organ on the roundabouts with majestic horses bobbing up and down and swingboats flying high, and much later in time there were dodgem cars.'

'May Day was an event. There was a one-day fair on Sarratt Green. Several days before, we children would make May baskets with wild flowers and sprigs of hay, with a doll dressed as the May Queen in the middle, and go "Maying" round the local houses on May Day morning, collecting pennies to spend at the fair. "Today, today is the very first of May, and the best time of the year," we sang, although the rest of the rhyme escapes me except for the line – "It's not much out but it's well spread about" referring to hawthorn twigs just budding.

We children would put our ears to the road on the evening before, to listen for Granny Bird's three steam engines coming, bringing the fair – we swore we could hear the vibrations. When they eventually reached Belsize, the women would alight from their horse-drawn dwelling vans with their babies and toddlers and go into my granny's cottage for tea and a chat and to show off their latest offspring. I was always slightly in awe of these women who seemed almost to speak a foreign language and were dressed in bright colours, with their hair in plaits around their head, and jangling ear-rings and beads.

Then, when the engines had toiled up the big hill towards Sarratt, "Toot toot" would sound, and off would go the women to catch up and set up the fair on Sarratt Green. "Fair Rock" which they boiled up, sticky and stripy, was a favourite sweet. Coconut shies, swing boats and a huge steam roundabout with prancing horses made

242

a magic world for an evening, and then off they would all go for a whole year before we listened for them again.

Before I was born, Belsize had a little fair of its own on Plough Monday.'

THE VILLAGE FETE AND FLOWER SHOW

'Years ago Shenley fete was always held on August Bank Holiday Monday and included many events which those visiting the show could take part in. One such event was Tilting the Bucket. This consisted of a course, at the end of which was a structure something like a goal (two uprights with a crossbar) and onto the crossbar was fixed a platform. Below the platform was a piece of wood with a hole in it and on top of the platform stood a bucket filled with water. This was an all male event and each team consisted of two people and a wheelbarrow. One wheeled the barrow in which sat his partner carrying a long wooden pole. The object of the exercise was to race down the course and at the far end aim the pole through the hole in the wood. Obviously, if one missed the hole, the pole would strike the board beneath the platform which would in turn, empty the bucket of water over the contestants.

A year that stands out in my memory was in the early 1920s. A number of lads had teamed up for Tilting the Bucket, but there was one hefty youth who could not find a partner. In desperation he came over to me to see if I would join in. Well, I was game to give it a go, so I dashed home to get my father's raincoat and a cap and came back suitably attired in case we got a dowsing! The course had to be run more than once and you had to alternate between being in the wheelbarrow and pushing it.

When it came to the final round my large partner was in the barrow, which I think had enough of his weight, and halfway down the course it broke! I wasn't going to be put off by a little thing like that so I staggered the rest of the way giving him a pick-a-back!

We actually won the event and at the end of the fete the prizes were presented by John Charrington. As we went up to collect ours there was a great cheer from the crowd but Mr Charrington held up his hand to quieten them and said that as this was an all male event, the prizes had been chosen appropriately and he gave me a cut-throat razor! He managed to say to me above the laughter that they would change it for something more suitable and I did eventually receive a pearl handled cake knife.'

'Bishops Stortford's Flower Show was quite an event in the 1920s and 1930s, held in the grounds of the Grange, the home of Sir John Barker, owner of Barker's, Derry & Toms, and Pontings in Kensington High Street. The sun always seemed to shine and we were dressed in our Sunday best with strict instructions never to get dirty. The marquees were filled with wonderful displays of fruit, vegetables and flowers – the perfume of the clarkia and mignonette still lingers in my memory. There were various stalls and entertainments, with the town band at the centre of it all.'

'The Flower Show was the highlight of the year. It was held in the park opposite Frogmore House, now no longer a park. We had a marquee and the competition was for a decorated dinner table. It sounds very ambitious but we thought it was lovely. Everything else paled before the sweet peas and silver.'

'A flower show was held in the summer at Burnham Green in the 1920s. The exhibits of flowers and vegetables were a sight to be seen – dahlias would be nearly as big as footballs, as would the onions. Sideshows were in abundance, and there was bowling for a pig. My dad looked after this. Practically all the men had nicknames and for some reason my dad was called "Punch" Archer, maybe it was his nose. A tug of war team from the village had great publicity, as did its football and cricket teams.'

THE CLUB TREAT

'My childhood was spent during the 1920s in the village of Stanstead Abbots near Ware. The highlight of the winter was the Club Treat which was held every January in the village Men's Club in the High Street. From just after 3pm – an hour before the doors were opened – a seething mass of children congregated in the forecourt, the atmosphere buzzing with excitement. We sat on forms at long trestle tables for our tea and had our fill of sandwiches and cakes with tea to drink. The club members always waited on us – I think their wives did all the dishing up and washing up in the kitchens. As the years progressed we did have ice cream, jelly and orange squash added to the menu.

Tea finished, tables were cleared and the forms arranged in front of the stage for the annual entertainment provided by the club members, female characters being performed by men. Whilst waiting for the entertainment to commence we raised the roof with our community singing.

On leaving the hall we were all given a present. My earliest recollection was the billiard room looking like Aladdin's cave with toys of every description piled high on the tables – the patience of the men as we made our selection! I recall mine was a doll's sewing machine that really stitched. We were also given a bun and an orange at the exit door. I think club members must have eventually decided this was too laborious a method of distributing our presents, as in the ensuing years we were presented with a grey voucher to the value of one shilling to be exchanged for goods at any of the village shops. As there was only one toy shop in the village (Hodgin's) I think

their small staff must have sympathised with the experience of the club members from previous years. There
were numerous toys in the shop priced at threepence and
sixpence so that we children had the choice of two or four
small gifts. On one occasion my selection, after nearly an
hour's deliberation, was a bag of marbles and paper
flowers that opened when immersed in water.

I do not recall when the Club Treat ceased although it
was not recommenced after the Second World War. I'm
sure there are still many inhabitants of Stanstead Abbots
who will be eternally grateful for the village club for
providing us with the treat which certainly brightened
our lives in the depression years of the 1920s.'

ALL THROUGH THE YEAR

Each year brought its annual pleasures, most still part of
our lives, though Empire Day, once enjoyed by every
schoolchild on 24th May, has gone the way of the British
Empire it celebrated. Christmas particularly was a magical time for children, as it still is, the smallest gift being a
treasure beyond price for those whose families struggled
through the year just to get by.

A CALENDAR OF CELEBRATION

'At Easter at Bayford we decorated the church with daffodils and primroses. We had Easter Egg Hunt parties,
searching for cardboard eggs with little eggs inside.

On Empire Day all the schoolchildren had to stand

246

around the flagpole to see the Union Jack hoisted and sing *God Save the King*.

Mr and Mrs Baker at Bayfordbury always gave a large Harvest Supper. Villagers brought all their produce, which was later given to Hertford Hospital. This stopped when the National Health Service took the hospital over in 1948. There was also Pound Day, when the villagers were asked to give a pound of anything they could spare and this was distributed to the very poor.'

'On Hospital Sunday at Welwyn, the Brownies, Guides etc walked in procession round the village behind the band. There was a church service and in the afternoon the gardens of the manor house were open to the public and the band played. I thought this was a wonderful day and all the money collected went to the hospital.'

'We had an early television set in 1947 at Letchworth but when anything interesting was on, such as the Boat Race, we couldn't see it for relations! Boat Race Day was well supported then, and we all wore pale blue or dark blue rosettes. Voting days too were lively, with all the children out booing or hooraying according to the party their parents favoured.'

'On May Day the village children at Park Street came to our back door with a hoop decorated with flowers and with a beautifully dressed doll sitting at the bottom. I think, and hope , they were well rewarded.'

'We had a pageant each Empire Day at Little Heath school, when to my annoyance I was always chosen to represent England (probably because of my rosy cheeks). I dearly longed to be from a more exotic country.'

247

'Burnham Green in the 1920s was a close knit community and nearly everyone was related in some way or another. Bonfire night was a big event, when a large bonfire would be built in the middle of the village green and various guys stuck on top. All the village turned out and we roasted chestnuts and potatoes.

Saints days were special and all the schoolchildren would march to Tewin church for a service and sometimes had a half day's holiday. On Remembrance Sunday we walked to Tewin and marched behind the British Legion to the service at the war memorial, which in those days took place on the 11th November at eleven o'clock and two minutes' silence was kept.'

CHRISTMASTIME

'Money was always short so we did not have the lovely presents that children have today. Nuts, tangerines or oranges and sweets filled our stocking, but we were given some wonderful parties. The WI provided a party in the village hall and a party was always held at Bayfordbury. Families lived close by and everyone got together and had a lot of fun and games.'

'Christmas was a landmark in the year. One clear memory is when my dad arrived home on Christmas Eve with a goose from Watford market – thankfully dead but fully clothed! My mum would have nothing to do with it, having already prepared a cockerel and pork, so dad and I had to pluck, draw and cook the bird. He knocked a hook into the wooden mantel over the fireplace, and suspended the goose on this, with a basin underneath to catch the dripping. All Christmas morning I sat there, Christmas Annual in one hand, big spoon in the other, and basted and turned that goose. My mum cooked the cockerel in the range in the kitchen and wouldn't touch our bird, but the next day when deep snow fell and stayed for a fortnight, we, and the rest of the row were glad of our goose.

Our Christmas shopping was done in Sarratt. Pink and white sugar mice from Alby Wingfield's, little chocolate sardines for the tree, and there were just two days off work and then life resumed as usual.'

'In the year 1910 when my late husband was six years of age, he sang his way into Hatfield church choir. That Christmas Eve, the choristers assembled in the church where they robed and were taken to Hatfield House to sing carols to the house party, guests of the then Lord and Lady Salisbury. When carols were finished the butler came in with lemonade, ginger-pop and hot mince pies. The great moment arrived when Lord Salisbury thanked the boys for the carols and gave each one a shilling. An awe inspiring experience to a little boy of six, and one he never ever forgot.'

'We had a large open fireplace in the main room at our farmhouse at Redbourn, where large logs could be burned. There were seats each side and the chimney was so wide one could look up and see the sky. At Christmas in the 1910s we hung our stockings there and on Christmas Eve the handbell ringers from Flamstead came and played carols while we sat round the hearth.'

'Pocket money could not be afforded by parents in the early years of the century so children had to work for it by stonepicking for roadworks, or acorn or potato picking. In season before 1914 at Libury Hall, which was then an Agricultural College for German students, we could go on Saturdays to pick soft fruit or shell peas and prepare beans for the cannery. The peas and beans brought ninepence a bushel, and the bushel was my day's work. This pocket money we were allowed to keep for our holiday or for special Christmas shopping. This was a Red Letter Day when we set off to walk five miles over the hill from Little Munden to the town, with a packed lunch for the journey and a bottle of cold tea to drink. We needed to be home by four or it would be dark. We came back with hidden secrets in our bags for Christmas presents for Mum, Dad, grandparents, brothers and sisters. The joy of giving was tremendous.'

'There would be great excitement on Christmas Eve when my dad along with all the other workers, received his present from the Estate. This was in the early 1920s. There would be a huge joint of beef – three pounds for Dad, two pounds for Mum and a pound each for us children. We all gathered round the big kitchen table to help unwrap it, mouths watering at the thought of a lovely helping the next day. From that, half would be cooked while the other half went in a big crock to be enjoyed the next week.'

'As a large family, with six children, we had lots of fun, especially at Christmastime. My eldest sister, 13 years my senior, always made sure that the younger ones had a good time. About a fortnight before Christmas she would take us from Hertford to Wood Green on the train. We would take our few coppers and buy small gifts for Mum and Dad. We were then taken to the Express Dairy in Turnpike Lane for a cream tea. She always decorated the tree on Christmas Eve and we were never allowed to see it until Christmas morning.'

'Boxing Day was always looked forward to in the 1920s at Burnham Green. The Hunt used to meet at Tewin Water House, the home of Sir Otto and Lady Beit. We would "run with them" all day and come home dog tired, having run many miles.'

Index

251